How to Read Literature Like a Professor:
For Kids

How to Read Literature Like a Professor: *For Kids*

Thomas C. Foster

HARPER
An Imprint of Harper Collins*Publishers*

"Landscape with Fall of Icarus" from *Pictures from Brueghel* by William Carlos Williams, copyright 1962 by New Directions Publishing, reprinted by permission of New Directions Publishing.

Excerpt from "Musée des Beaux Arts" from *Collected Poems* by W. H. Auden, copyright 1940, 1976 by Random House, reprinted by permission of Random House.

 For information address HarperCollins Children's Books, a division of HarperCollins Publishers, 195 Broadway, New York, NY 10007.
www.harpercollinschildrens.com

Library of Congress Control Number: 2013933033
ISBN 978-0-06-220086-0 (trade bdg.)
ISBN 978-0-06-220085-3 (pbk.)

Typography by Erich Nagler
22 23 24 25 26 LSB 9 8 7 6 5

❖

First Edition

For my sons, Robert and Nathan

CONTENTS

INTRODUCTION

How'd He Do That?

MR. *LINDNER? THAT wimp?*

Right. Mr. Lindner, the wimp. So what did you think the devil would look like? If he were red with a tail, horns, and cloven hooves, any fool would know to turn down his offer.

The class and I are discussing Lorraine Hansberry's play *A Raisin in the Sun* (1959). The confused questions arise when I suggest that Mr. Lindner is the devil.

The Youngers, an African-American family in Chicago, have made a down payment on a house in an all-white neighborhood. Mr. Lindner, a meek little man, has come to visit with a check in hand. He (along with all the neighbors) wants the family to take the check and move right back out again.

At first Walter Lee Younger confidently turns down the offer. He believes that the family's money (a life insurance payment they received after the death of Walter's father) is secure. But shortly after sending Mr. Lindner away, he discovers that two-thirds of that money has been stolen. All of a sudden Mr. Lindner's insulting offer comes to look like the family's salvation.

Bargains with the devil go a long way back. Most take the form of the Faust legend. In this old story, the devil offers Faust a life of pleasure, riches, and power, in return for his soul. Faust accepts happily, enjoys his good times, and then repents too late as the devil drags his dying soul to hell. It's a story that's retold often. Each time, the hero is offered something he desperately wants—power or knowledge or a fastball that will beat the Yankees—and all he has to give up is his soul.

In Hansberry's version, when Mr. Lindner makes his offer, he doesn't mention Walter Lee's soul. He doesn't even know that he is demanding it. He is, though. Walter Lee can be rescued from his family's crisis. All he has to do is to admit that he's not equal to his new white neighbors, that his pride and self-respect, his *identity*, can be bought.

If that's not selling your soul, what is?

But Walter Lee resists the devil's temptation. He looks at himself and at the true cost of the bargain and recovers in time to reject the devil's—Mr. Lindner's—offer. Walter Lee grows into a hero as he wrestles with his own demons as well as with the one who comes to visit with a check, and he comes through without falling. His soul is still his own.

SOMETHING ALWAYS HAPPENS in this conversation between professor and students. Each of us gets a look on our faces. My look says, "What, you don't get it?" Theirs says, "We don't get it. And we think you're making it up." Basically, we've all read the same story, but we haven't used the same tools to analyze it.

It might seem as if the teacher is inventing a way to interpret the story out of thin air. Actually, the teacher just has some more experience. And the teacher has gathered, over the years, a kind of "grammar of literature." That's a certain set of patterns, codes, and rules that we can learn to use when we're reading a piece of writing.

Stories and novels have a very large set of conventions, or rules, or things that you can learn to expect: types of characters, plot rhythms, chapter structures, points of view. Poems have a great many conventions of their own. Plays, too. And there are certain conventions that show up in all three. Spring usually means the same thing, whether it's mentioned in a poem or a play or a novel. So does snow. So does darkness. So does sleep.

Whenever spring is mentioned, we all start to think of the same ideas: youth, promise, young lambs, children skipping . . . on and on. And if we keep thinking, we might get to other concepts, like new birth, new life, renewal.

Okay, let's say you're right and there is a set of conventions, like a key to reading literature. How do I get so I can recognize these?

Same way you get to Carnegie Hall. Practice.

When readers first read a piece of fiction, they focus on the story and the characters: who are these people, what are they doing, and what wonderful or terrible things are happening to them? They will respond emotionally, with joy or horror, laughter or tears, anxiety or delight. This is what every author hopes for.

But when an English teacher reads, though he will respond emotionally as well, a lot of his attention will also be fixed on other things. It will be asking other questions. Where did that joy or grief or anxiety *come* from? Does this character seem like any others I've read about? Where have I seen this situation before? If you learn to ask these questions, you'll read and understand literature in a new light. And it will become even more rewarding and fun.

CHAPTER ONE

Every Trip Is a Quest (Except When It's Not)

OKAY, SO HERE'S the deal: let's say you're reading a book about an average sixteen-year-old kid in the summer of 1968. The kid—let's call him Kip Smith, who hopes his acne clears up before he gets drafted—is on his way to the A&P to get a loaf of bread. His bike is a one-speed with a coaster brake and therefore very embarrassing to ride, and riding it to run an errand for his mother makes it worse. Along the way he has a couple of disturbing experiences, including an unpleasant encounter with a German shepherd. And it's all topped off in the supermarket parking lot when he sees the girl of his dreams, Karen, laughing and fooling around in Tony Vauxhall's brand-new car, a Barracuda.

Now, Kip hates Tony already because he's got a name like Vauxhall and not Smith, and because the Barracuda is bright green and goes approximately the speed of light, and also because Tony has never had to work a day in his life. Karen, who is laughing and having a great time, turns and sees Kip, who asked her out not so long ago. And she keeps laughing.

Kip goes on into the store to buy the loaf of Wonder Bread that his mother told him to pick up. As he reaches for the bread, he decides right then and there to lie about his age to the Marine recruiter, even though it means going to Vietnam, because nothing will ever happen to him if he stays in this one-horse town where the only thing that matters is how much money your father has.

What just happened here?

If you were an English teacher, and not even a particularly weird English teacher, you'd know that you'd just watched a knight have an encounter with his enemy.

In other words, a quest just happened.

But it just looked like a trip to the store for some white bread.

True. But think about it. What is a quest made of? A knight, a dangerous road, a Holy Grail, at least one dragon, one evil knight, one princess. Sounds about right? That's a list I can live with. We've got a knight (named Kip), a dangerous road (nasty German shepherd), a Holy Grail (a loaf of Wonder Bread), at least one dragon (trust me, a '68 Barracuda could definitely breathe fire), one evil knight (Tony), one princess (Karen).

Seems like a bit of a stretch.

At first, sure. But let's think about what a quest is made of. It needs five things:

1. a quester;
2. a place to go;
3. a stated reason to go there;
4. challenges and trials along the way;
5. a real reason to go there.

Item 1 is easy; a quester is just a person who goes on a quest, whether or not he knows it's a quest. In fact, he usually doesn't know. Items 2 and 3 go together: someone tells our main character, our *hero,* to go somewhere and do something. Go in search of the Holy Grail. Go to the store for some bread. Go to Mount Doom and throw in a ring. Go there, do that.

Now remember that I said the *stated* reason for the quest. That's because of item 5.

The real reason for the quest is *never* the same as the stated reason. In fact, more often than not, the quester fails at the stated task. (Frodo makes it all the way to Mount Doom, but does he throw the ring in the fire? No, he does not. Really—go read it again if you don't believe me.) So why do heroes go on these quests, and why do we care? They go because of the stated task, believing that it is their real mission. We know, however, that their quest is educational. They don't know enough about the only subject that really matters: themselves. **The real reason for a quest is *always* self-knowledge.**

Frodo may have saved the world from Sauron, but that really just turned out to be a bit of luck. What his quest actually brings him is a new understanding of the value of mercy and who needs it: Gollum, Frodo himself, and probably everybody in Middle Earth.

Or here's another example. You know the book, I'm sure: *How the Grinch Stole Christmas* (1957).

Wait a minute. The Grinch *is on a quest?*

Sure. Here's the setup:

1. *Our quester:* a grumpy, cave-dwelling creature who's had it up to here with the noise, celebration, and general happiness of Christmas.
2. *A place to go:* from his mountaintop cave to the village of Whoville, far below.
3. *A stated reason to go there:* to steal every Christmas present, tree, and bit of decoration he can lay his hands on.
4. *Challenges and trials:* a risky sleigh trip down the mountain, considerable effort packing up the Christmas presents and trimmings, an encounter with a two-year-old girl who puts all

the Grinch's efforts in peril simply by asking a question, and a painfully difficult trip back up the mountain with an overloaded sleigh.

5. *The real reason to go:* to learn what Christmas actually means, to have his shriveled heart expand back to its proper size (or even bigger), and to find genuine happiness.

Once you get the hang of it, you can see how *How the Grinch Stole Christmas* follows the conventions of a quest tale. So does *The Lord of the Rings. Huckleberry Finn. Star Wars. Holes.* And most other stories of someone going somewhere and doing something, especially if the going and the doing weren't the protagonist's idea in the first place.

A word of warning: if I sometimes speak here and in the chapters to come as if a certain statement is always true, I apologize. "Always" and "never" are not words that have much meaning when it comes to literature. For one thing, as soon as something seems to always be true, some wise guy will come along and write something to prove that it's not.

Let's think about journeys. Sometimes the quest fails or is not taken up by the protagonist. And is every trip really a quest? It depends. Some days I just drive to work—no adventures, no growth. I'm sure that the same is true in writing. Sometimes plot requires that a writer get a character from home to work and back again. But still, when a character hits the road, we should start to pay attention, just to see if, you know, something's going on there.

Once you figure out quests, the rest is easy.

CHAPTER TWO

Nice to Eat with You: Acts of Communion

Sometimes a meal is just a meal. Characters in books can get hungry just like people outside of books. More often, though, it's not. In books, whenever people eat or drink together, it's communion.

Communion has for many readers one and only one meaning. While that meaning is very important, it is not the only one. Nor does Christianity have a lock on the practice. Nearly every religion has some kind of ritual where the faithful come together to share nourishment. But not all communions are holy. In books, there are quite a few kinds of communion.

Here's the thing to remember about communions of all kinds: in the real world, breaking bread together is an act of sharing and peace, since if you're breaking bread, you're generally not breaking heads. You usually invite your friends to dinner, not your enemies. In fact, we're quite particular about who we eat with. Generally, eating with someone is a way of saying, "I'm with you, I like you, we form a community together." And that is a kind of communion.

So it is in literature. And in literature, there is another reason. Writing a meal scene is so difficult, and basically so *dull* (what can you say about fried chicken that hasn't already been said?), that there really needs to be some very important reason to include one in the story. And that reason has to do with how the characters are getting along. Or not getting along.

How about the main character (who doesn't even have a name) of Dr. Seuss's *Green Eggs and Ham* (1960)? He doesn't want to eat green eggs and ham. Not even to try them. *And* he doesn't want to listen to the little creature named Sam coaxing and begging and nagging him to take just one bite. In fact, he wants Sam to go away. "You let me be!" he orders Sam. But when he finally does give in and try, he likes green eggs and ham—and he even likes Sam. He eats, and he gains a friend. Communion at its simplest.

Sometimes just meaning or planning to share some food is all that the story needs—you don't actually have to see the characters taking a single bite. Roald Dahl's *Charlie and the Chocolate Factory* (1964) is all about eating, even though it starts out as one of the hungriest books out there. Charlie and his family live on bread, potatoes, and cabbage, and not enough of any of it. They are slowly starving.

There is love in this downtrodden family, though, and the person poor little Charlie loves the most is his grandpa Joe. Grandpa Joe gives Charlie all the money he has in the world: a dime. Charlie uses the dime to buy (what else?) a chocolate bar. And Charlie and Grandpa Joe share the experience of hesitantly, almost fearfully, peeling off the wrapper to see if, underneath, they will find the golden ticket that will let them into Willy Wonka's fabulous chocolate factory.

They don't find it. They find only a chocolate bar.

And they both burst out laughing.

They don't have to take a bite of the candy for readers to see what these two characters share. They share the sense of fun, of excitement, and of possibility that is a part of childhood. They share laughter. They share *hope.* Their communion over the bar of Willy Wonka's chocolate brings them closer than ever, and the old man and the little boy spend the rest of the book at each other's side.

What about when characters don't eat together? What if a meal turns ugly or doesn't happen at all?

There's a different outcome, but the same logic. If a tasty meal or snack or a delicious bar of chocolate suggests that good things will happen between the people who share it, then a meal that doesn't work out is a bad sign. It happens all the time on television shows. Two people are at dinner and a third comes up, and one or both of the first two refuse to eat. They place their napkins on their plates, or say something about having lost their appetites, and walk away. Immediately we know what they think about the intruder.

Consider another book about chocolate: Robert Cormier's *The Chocolate War* (1974). Well, the title *says* the book is about chocolate. Actually the book is about bullying. And corruption. And power. About what it takes—and what it *costs*—to stand up to people with power. Jerry Renault defies the students who control his school by refusing to sell chocolates for a fund-raiser, and he is destroyed for that choice. No one supports him. He's on his own.

Nobody eats, either. In an entire book about chocolate, nobody tastes one mouthful. There is no eating, there is no communion, and there is no help for Jerry. If anybody had ever cracked open a box of those fund-raiser chocolates and taken a bite, the poor kid might have had a chance.

CHAPTER THREE

Nice to Eat You: Acts of Vampires

WHAT A DIFFERENCE one little word makes! If you take the "with" out of "Nice to eat with you," it begins to mean something quite different. Less wholesome. More creepy. It just goes to show that not all eating that happens in literature is friendly. Not only that, it doesn't even always look like eating. Beyond here, there be monsters.

Vampires in literature, you say? Big deal. I've read *Twilight. Dracula.* Anne Rice.

Good for you. Everyone deserves a good scare—or a good swoon. But actual vampires are only the beginning. Not only that, they're not even necessarily the most alarming. After all, you can at least recognize a vampire who has fangs.

Let's start with Dracula himself. You know how in all those Dracula movies, or almost all, the count has this weird attractiveness to him? Sometimes he's downright sexy. Always, he's dangerous, mysterious, and he tends to focus on beautiful, unmarried women. And when he gets them, he grows younger, more alive (if we can say this of the undead). Meanwhile, his victims become like him and begin to seek out their own victims.

Now let's think about this for a moment. A nasty old man, attractive but evil, violates young women, leaves his mark on them, steals their innocence, and leaves them helpless followers in his sin. I think we'd be reasonable to conclude that the whole Count Dracula story is up to something more than merely scaring us out of our wits. In fact, we might conclude that it has something to do with sex.

But what about vampires who never bite?

You're right—famously, Edward does not bite Bella. But the vampire hero of Stephenie Meyer's *Twilight* (2005) is mysteriously and powerfully attractive, isn't he? (Just like Dracula.) And he *wants* to bite Bella, doesn't he? (Just like Dracula.) Edward may be different in his self-control, but not in his desire. He wants exactly what Dracula wants—the blood of an innocent young woman. A young woman whose bedroom he creeps into. A young woman he watches while she sleeps.

So vampirism isn't about vampires?

Oh, it is. It is. But it's also about other things: selfishness, exploitation, a refusal to accept that other people have the right to exist, just for starters. We'll come back to this list a little later on.

This rule also applies to other scary favorites, such as ghosts or doppelgängers (ghost doubles or evil twins). Ghosts are always about something besides themselves. Think of the ghost of Hamlet's father, when he takes to appearing on the castle ramparts at midnight. He's not there simply to haunt his son; he's there to point out something seriously wrong in Denmark's royal household. (What's wrong? Oh, just that the king's brother first murdered the king and then married his widow.)

Or consider Marley's ghost in *A Christmas Carol* (1843), who is really a walking, clanking, moaning lesson in ethics for Scrooge. Or take Dr. Jekyll's other half. In *The Strange Case of Dr. Jekyll and Mr. Hyde* (1886), Robert Louis Stevenson uses the hideous Mr. Hyde to show readers that even a respectable man has a dark side. Writers use ghosts, vampires, werewolves, and all manner of scary things to symbolize certain things about our everyday existence.

Ghosts and vampires are never only about ghosts and vampires.

Here's where it gets a little tricky, though: the ghosts and vampires don't always have to appear in visible form. Sometimes the really scary bloodsuckers are entirely human.

Henry James has a famous story, "Daisy Miller" (1878), in which there are no ghosts, there is no demonic possession—there's nothing more mysterious than a midnight jaunt to the Colosseum in Rome. Daisy is a young American woman who does as she pleases. She upsets the social customs of the rich Europeans she meets. Eventually, Daisy dies, apparently because she caught malaria on her trip to the Colosseum. But you know what actually kills her? Vampires.

No, really. Vampires. I know I told you there weren't any supernatural forces at work here. But you don't need fangs and a cape to be a vampire.

Daisy wants the attention of a man named Winterbourne. Winterbourne and his aunt and their circle of friends watch Daisy and disapprove of her. But because of a hunger to disapprove of something, they never cut her loose entirely. Instead, they play with her yearning to become one of them. At last, Winterbourne spots Daisy with a (male) friend at the Colosseum at night and pretends not to see her. Daisy says, "He cuts me dead!" That should be clear enough for anybody.

The important points of the vampire story are all here. There's an older man who represents corrupt, worn-out values. There's a fresh, innocent young woman. The woman loses her youth, energy, and virtue.

The older man continues to live. The young woman dies.

There are books, of course, where the ghost or vampire is just a cheap thrill, without any particular meaning. But such works tend not to have much staying power in readers' minds. We're haunted only while we're reading. In the books that continue to haunt us, however, the figure of the vampire, the cannibal, the spook, shows up again and again, whenever someone grows in strength by weakening someone else.

That's what the vampire figure really comes down to: using other people to get what we want. Denying someone else's right to live. Placing our own desires, particularly our ugly ones, above the needs of someone else. My guess is that as long as people act in selfish ways, the vampire will be with us.

CHAPTER FOUR

If It's Square, It's a Sonnet

Every now and then, I'll ask my students what kind of poem we're talking about—what *form* the poem uses. The first time, the answer will be "sonnet." The next time, "sonnet." Care to guess about the third? Very good. Basically, I figure the sonnet is the only poetic form most readers will ever need to know. It's very common, has been written in every time period since the English Renaissance, and is still popular today.

After I tell the students the first time that the poem is a sonnet, someone asks me how I knew so fast. I tell them two things. First, that I read the poem before class (useful for someone in my position, or theirs, come to think of it). And second, that I counted the lines when I noticed the shape of the poem. It's square. The miracle of the sonnet, you see, is that it is fourteen lines long and most lines have ten syllables. And ten syllables of English are about as long as fourteen lines are high. Square.

Okay, great. Who cares?

I agree, up to a point. I think people who read poems should always read the poem first, without even thinking about its form or its style. They should not begin by counting lines or looking at line endings to find the rhyme scheme. Just enjoy the experience.

After you've had that first experience, though, one of the extra pleasures you can get is seeing *how* the poet worked that magic on you. There are many ways a poem can charm the reader: choice of images, music of the language, idea content, wordplay. And form.

You might think that a poem of a mere fourteen lines is only capable of doing one thing. But you'd be wrong. A sonnet, in fact, has two units of meaning, and a shift takes place between the first and the second. These two units are closely related to the two parts of the sonnet. And it's the sonnet's form that creates those two parts.

Most sonnets have one group of eight lines and one of six. (You can have a Petrarchan sonnet, which has an octave—eight lines—and a sestet, a group of six. Or a Shakespearean sonnet, which has three groups of four lines—three quatrains—and a couplet, two lines. But even there, the first two quatrains join up to make a group of eight lines, and the last quatrain joins up with the couplet to make of group of six.) However it works, the basic pattern is 8/6.

Let's look at an example.

Christina Rossetti was a British poet of the late 1800s. This is her poem "An Echo from Willow-Wood" (about 1870). I suggest you read it out loud, to get the full effect.

Two gazed into a pool, he gazed and she,
Not hand in hand, yet heart in heart, I think,
Pale and reluctant on the water's brink,
As on the brink of parting which must be.
Each eyed the other's aspect, she and he,
Each felt one hungering heart leap up and sink,
Each tasted bitterness which both must drink,
There on the brink of life's dividing sea.
Lilies upon the surface, deep below
Two wistful faces craving each for each,
Resolute and reluctant without speech:—
A sudden ripple made the faces flow,
One moment joined, to vanish out of reach:
So those hearts joined, and ah were parted so.

It's a terrific little poem in its own right, and a good poem for our purposes. For one thing, it has neither a thee nor a thou in sight, so we get rid of some of the confusion that older poetry slings at modern readers. Anyway, I like Christina Rossetti, and I think that more people should be able to fall in love with her.

At first glance the poem doesn't really look square. True, but it's close. So the first question is: how many sentences? (Not lines, of which there are fourteen, but sentences.) The answer is three.

Can you guess where one period falls? Right. End of line eight.

The first eight lines, the octave, carry one idea. In this case, it's two sentences of four lines each (which we call quatrains). This is pretty common. The last six lines, the sestet, carry another related idea. In the octave, Rossetti creates a still, unmoving picture of two lovers right before some kind of event. Everything in it points to how they are about to go away from each other. They are "on the brink of parting which must be." And yet, with all this anxiety and fear—full of "hungering" and "bitterness"—their surface, like that of the water, is calm. Inside, their hearts may leap up and sink, yet they show nothing, since they don't even look at each other, but only at each other's reflection in the water.

In the sestet, though, a puff of breeze creates a ripple and dissolves that carefully controlled image. The water, which has brought them—or their reflections—together, now pulls them apart. What is possible in the octave (the separation of the lovers) becomes real in the sestet.

Without making any extravagant claims—no, this is not the greatest sonnet ever written—we can say that "An Echo from Willow-Wood" is an excellent example of its form. Rossetti tells a story of human longing and regret within the boundaries of fourteen lines. The beauty of this poem lies, in part, in the tension between the small package and the large emotions it contains. We feel that the story is in danger of breaking out of its vessel, but of course it never does. The vessel, the sonnet form, actually becomes part of the meaning of the poem.

And this is why form matters, and why teachers pay attention to it: it just might mean something. When a poet chooses to write a sonnet instead of, say, something on the scope of John Milton's *Paradise Lost*, it's not because he or she is lazy. Short poems take far more time per line, because everything has to be perfect, than long ones.

We owe it to poets, I think, to notice that they've gone to this trouble. And we owe it to ourselves to understand the nature of the thing we're reading. When you start to read a poem, then, look at the shape.

CHAPTER FIVE

Now Where Have I Seen Him Before?

ONE OF THE many great things about being an English teacher is that you get to keep meeting old friends. For beginning readers, though, every story may seem new. Each book feels unconnected to any other book. It's like one of those pictures where you connect the dots. When I was a kid, I could never see the picture in a connect-the-dots drawing until I'd put in nearly every line. Other kids could look at a page full of dots and say, "Oh, that's an elephant." Me, I saw dots.

Part of this is just how good you happen to be at seeing two-dimensional pictures. But a lot of it is practice. The more connect-the-dots drawings you do, the more likely you are to recognize the picture early on.

Same with literature. Part of pattern recognition is talent, but a whole lot of it is practice. If you read enough, and think enough about what you read, you'll begin to see patterns: things that happen again and again.

It may pay to remember this: **there's no such thing as a completely original work of literature.**

Once you know that, you can go looking for old friends and asking the question: "Now where have I seen him (or her) before?"

Take Bod, the hero of Neil Gaiman's *The Graveyard Book* (2008). Bod is very young, still in diapers, when he's left an orphan. Accidentally, cheerfully, in fact, he wanders into a haunted graveyard. He's too young to know that cemeteries, tombstones, and ghosts are supposed to be scary, so he's not scared. The ghosts see him for what he is—a child who needs a family. They give him one; they take him in. The graveyard becomes his home. And the graveyard's solitary, brooding vampire becomes young Bod's guardian, carefully keeping him safe against all the perils of the outside world until he's old enough to face them on his own.

Now, forget all the details about graveyards, ghosts, and vampires, and think of Bod as a type. A very young orphaned boy, all on his own in a scary and threatening place. A human boy taken in by a group of nonhumans, with a protective and mysterious guardian who is also not human. Have you met him before?

You have if you know Rudyard Kipling's *The Jungle*

Book (1894), where the human boy Mowgli is raised by wolves and watched over by a black panther. Put an orphan boy who needs a family in the jungle, and you have *The Jungle Book*. Put him in a graveyard, and you have *The Graveyard Book*. Even the book's title is a big clue. Neil Gaiman not only used Kipling's story on purpose; he wanted readers to know that's what he was doing.

Which brings us to the big secret: **there's only one story.**

There, I said it, and I can't very well take it back. There is only one story. Ever. One. It's always been going on and it's everywhere around us and every story you've ever read or heard of or watched is part of it. *The Thousand and One Nights*. Harry Potter. "Jack and the Beanstalk." *Romeo and Juliet. The Simpsons.*

To me, literature is something like a barrel of eels. When a writer creates a new eel, it wriggles its way into the barrel. It's a new eel, but it shares its eelness with all those other eels that are in the barrel or have ever been in the barrel. Now, if that doesn't put you off reading entirely, you know you're serious.

But the point is this: stories grow out of other stories, poems out of other poems. Of course poems can learn from plays, songs from novels. Sometimes the influence is direct and obvious, as it is with *The Graveyard Book*. Other times it's less direct and more subtle. Maybe a modern-day miser makes the reader think of

Scrooge. A female character may remind us of Scarlett O'Hara or Ophelia or Pocahontas. After much practice of reading, you begin to notice these similarities.

All this "books look like other books" is all well and good, but what does it mean for our reading?

Excellent question. If we don't see the reference, the connection, then it means nothing, right? Which isn't bad. If you don't know *The Jungle Book* and you don't realize that Neil Gaiman was using it when he wrote *The Graveyard Book,* you can still enjoy the novel on its own. It's a fun story, it works, and it gives pleasure to its readers. From there, everything else that happens is a bonus.

But if you *do* realize that *The Graveyard Book* refers to *The Jungle Book,* you get more. A small part of this is what I call the *aha!* factor. It's the delight we feel at recognizing something familiar, something we've met before. *Aha!* Bod is Mowgli. We get it.

That moment of pleasure, wonderful as it is, is not enough on its own. Once we notice a similarity, it leads us forward. We begin to draw comparisons and parallels between the two books. We begin to think about what it means that Bod is in a graveyard, while Mowgli is in a jungle. We begin to think about wilderness and what it might mean. And we begin to think even more about the big point Kipling and Gaiman are both making: what does it say about people in general that a pack of wolves, or a group of ghosts, must take in a human baby and keep him safe? When home is a jungle or a graveyard, when animals or monsters become family, what does that mean about the people and communities that are *supposed* to create homes for Mowgli and for Bod?

Well, what does *it say? What does it mean?*

I'm not going to tell you. But the point is, once you realize that *The Graveyard Book* and *The Jungle Book* are connected, you can ask these questions in new ways, and you have new places to hunt for the answers.

This conversation, back and forth between old books and new, is always going on. It makes the experience of reading books deeper and richer. The more we notice that the book we're reading is speaking to other books, the more similarities we begin to notice, and the more alive the text becomes.

But what do we do if we don't see all these similarities?

First of all, don't worry. If a story is no good, being based on *Hamlet* won't save it. The characters have to work as characters, as themselves. Silas the vampire needs to be a great character, which he is, before we need to worry about his resemblance to Bagheera the black panther. If the story is good and the characters work, but you don't notice the ways it connects to an older book, then you've done nothing worse than read a good story with characters you will remember. If you begin to pick up on some of these connections, however, you'll find that your understanding of the novel becomes deeper and more meaningful.

But we haven't read everything.

Neither have I. Nor has anyone. Young readers, of course, have a slightly harder time, which is why teachers are useful in pointing out things you might have missed or didn't know to look for. When I was a kid, I used to go mushroom hunting with my father. I would never see them, but he'd say, "There's a yellow sponge," or "There are a couple of black spikes." And because I knew they were there, my looking would become more focused. In a few moments, I would begin seeing them for myself. And once you begin seeing mushrooms, you can't stop. What an English teacher does is very similar; he tells you when you get near mushrooms. Once you know that, you can hunt for mushrooms on your own.

CHAPTER SIX

When in Doubt, It's from Shakespeare . . .

IF YOU LOOK at any literary period between the eighteenth and twenty-first centuries, you'll be amazed by how much Shakespeare you find. He's everywhere, in every form you can think of. And he's never the same: every age and every writer reinvents its own Shakespeare.

Woody Allen took *A Midsummer Night's Dream* and made it into his film *A Midsummer Night's Sex Comedy*. Naturally.

The BBC series *Masterpiece* has redone *Othello* as the story of black police commissioner John Othello, his lovely white wife, Dessie, and his friend Ben Jago, who resents the fact that he was not picked for promotion.

If you know that Shakespeare's Othello is manipulated by his jealous friend, Iago, into murdering his wife, Desdemona, then you won't be surprised if things go badly for John, Dessie, and Ben as well.

West Side Story (1957) famously reworks *Romeo and Juliet* (about 1591–95), as two doomed lovers are parted by prejudice and violence. *Romeo + Juliet* also became a movie in the 1990s, featuring hip teen culture and automatic pistols. And that's a century or so after Tchaikovsky's ballet based on the same play. Then there is Sharon M. Draper's *Romiette and Julio* (1999), about two teenagers falling deeply in love. But a dangerous local gang is firmly opposed to an African-American girl and a Latino boy dating each other, and soon Romiette and Julio's relationship—and their lives—are at risk.

Hamlet comes out as a new film every couple of years, it seems. Tom Stoppard takes two minor characters from *Hamlet* and gives them an entire play of their own in *Rosencrantz and Guildenstern Are Dead.* And the 1960s TV series *Gilligan's Island* even had an episode in which the characters put together a musical *Hamlet.* Now that's art.

Those are just a few of the uses to which Shakespeare's plots and situations get put. But if that's all he amounted to, he'd only be a little different from any other immortal writer.

But that's not all.

You know what's great about reading old Will? You keep stumbling across lines you've been hearing and reading all your life. Try these:

- *To thine own self be true.*
- *All the world's a stage*
  And all the men and women merely players.
- *What's in a name? That which we call a rose*
  By any other name would smell as sweet.
- *Good night, sweet prince,*
  And flights of angels sing thee to thy rest!
- *Get thee to a nunnery.*
- *A horse! a horse! My kingdom for a horse!*
- *Double, double, toil and trouble*
  Fire burn and cauldron bubble.
- *By the pricking of my thumbs*
  Something wicked this way comes.

Oh, and lest I forget:

- *To be, or not to be, that is the question.*

Ever heard any of those? This week? Today? In my copy of *Bartlett's Familiar Quotations,* Shakespeare takes up forty-seven pages. My first guess is that you probably have not read most of the plays from which these quotations are taken; my second guess is that you knew at least some of the phrases anyway.

All right, so Shakespeare is always with us. What does that mean?

He means something to us as readers in part because he means so much to our writers. So let's consider why writers turn to our man.

It makes them sound smarter?

Smarter than what?

Than quoting Rocky and Bullwinkle, *for instance.*

Careful. I'm a big fan of Moose and Squirrel. Still, I take your point. There are a lot of things to quote that don't sound as good as Shakespeare. Almost all of them, in fact.

Plus it shows that you've read him, right? It shows that you're an educated person.

Not necessarily. I could have given you Richard III's famous request for a horse since I was nine. My father was a great fan of that play, so I heard that famous line ("A horse! A horse! My kingdom for a horse!") early on. My dad was a factory worker with a high school education. He wasn't particularly interested in impressing anybody with his fancy learning. He was pleased, however, to be able to talk about these great stories, these plays he had read and loved.

We love the plays, the great characters, the fabulous speeches, the witty comebacks. I hope never to be stabbed, but if I am, I'd sure like to be able to answer, when somebody asks me if it's bad, "No, 'tis not so deep as a well, nor so wide as a church door; but 'tis enough, 'twill serve," as Mercutio does in *Romeo and Juliet.* I mean, to be dying and clever at the same time, how can you not love that?

Rather than saying that quoting Shakespeare proves you're smart, I think what happens is that writers quote what they've read or heard. And they have more Shakespeare stuck in their heads than anyone else. (Except, of course, Bugs Bunny.)

But there's something else you may not have thought of. Shakespeare is also someone writers can struggle against, or bounce their ideas off. It's worth remembering that few writers simply copy bits of Shakespeare's work into their own. More commonly, they take a little from the older work while also letting their own newer work have its say. The new writer has his own agenda, his own slant to put on things.

In *Romeo and Juliet,* both the young lovers commit suicide. In *West Side Story,* Tony is murdered but Maria survives. In *Romiette and Julio,* both teens live to the end of the book. Each ending says different things about the characters, their families and communities, and their attitudes (and the reader's attitudes) toward life and death. Each asks readers to think about what a tragedy is. And each one is even more interesting if you think, not just about the modern movie or book, but about the four-hundred-year-old play that inspired it.

That's what writers can do with Shakespeare. Of course, they can do it with other writers as well, and they do, but not quite as often. Why? You know why. The stories are great, the characters compelling, the language fabulous. And we know him. You can base your new work on Fulke Greville if you like, but you'd have to provide footnotes.

So what's in it for readers? When we recognize the connections between Shakespeare and something new we are reading, we bring our own knowledge to the story. We become partners with the writer in creating meaning. Even before we start reading, we know some of what the writer wants us to know—for example, that Tony and Maria or Romiette and Julio will face danger because of their love for each other. We know it because Shakespeare has already told us.

Our understanding of both works becomes richer and deeper when we see the connections between them. We figure out something about the newer work. Maybe even see the old one with new eyes.

And the writer we know better than any other, the one whose language and whose plays we "know" even if we haven't read him, the one it's easiest and most rewarding for a writer to use in this way—is Shakespeare.

CHAPTER SEVEN

. . . Or the Bible

CONNECT THESE DOTS: garden, serpent, plagues, flood, parting of waters, loaves, fishes, forty days, betrayal, denial, slavery and escape, fatted calves, milk and honey. Ever read a book with all these things in them?

Guess what? So have your writers. Poets. Playwrights. Screenwriters.

Maybe a writer doesn't need characters, theme, or a plot, but just a title. The Bible is full of possible titles. James Dean starred in the famous movie *East of Eden*. (Why east? Because John Steinbeck, who wrote the story on which the film is based, knew his Genesis. To find yourself east of Eden is to be outside of the garden, in a fallen world. Which is the only kind of world we know, and certainly the only kind there could be in a James Dean movie.) William Faulkner has *Absalom, Absalom!* (1936) and *Go Down, Moses* (1942). (Okay, that last one's from a spiritual, but the song itself is about a biblical story.) Suppose you want to write about one sister who can't seem to win any love or recognition from her family and another sister everyone adores. You might turn to a biblical story of two brothers and call your book *Jacob Have I Loved* (1981), as Katherine Paterson did.

Poetry is absolutely full of Scripture. John Milton took most of his subjects from you-know-where: *Paradise Lost* (1667), *Paradise Regained, Samson Agonistes* (both 1671). Those questing knights in the anonymous late-fourteenth-century *Sir Gawain and the Green Knight* and Edmund Spenser's *The Faerie Queen* (1590–1596) are searching on behalf of their religion, whether they know it or not (and they usually do know). Even Geoffrey Chaucer's pilgrims in *The Canterbury Tales* (1384) are making an Easter pilgrimage to Canterbury Cathedral. Neither they nor their tales are particularly holy, but much of their talk involves the Bible and religious teachings.

Some serious Bible stories turn comic in the hands of a modern writer. In Eudora Welty's story "Why I Live at the P.O." (1941), the narrator is in the grips of sibling rivalry. Her younger sister has just arrived back in her family's town, daughter in tow. The narrator is outraged because she has to cook two chickens to feed five grown-ups and a small child just because her "spoiled" younger sister has come home. What Sister can't see, but we can, is that those two birds are really a fatted calf. It may not be the grandest feast ever cooked, but it definitely *is* a feast, and a feast is what you have to have when the Prodigal Son comes home. Even if the Prodigal Son turns out to be a daughter.

Okay, so there are a lot of ways the Bible shows up. But isn't that a problem for anyone who isn't exactly . . .

A Bible scholar? Well, I'm not. But even I can sometimes recognize when a writer is making use of something from the Bible. Here's how it works.

Four children make their way through a mysterious wardrobe into a magical land. This land is in the grip of perpetual winter and ruled by a cruel and selfish witch. But there is hope that a savior will come, hope that these four children will somehow bring that savior to this frozen wasteland.

This might seem like the setup for many a fantasy novel. Children often make journeys to fantastic, magical places. There are often evil witches or other villains who need to be defeated. But when one of the children gives in to temptation and betrays the others to the witch; and when the savior offers his own life in return for the life of the traitor; and when two of the children stay awake to talk with the savior on the night before his death—you can start to see some parallels to the Bible, can't you? And when the savior is actually killed and then *comes back to life*, you know we're not just talking about Narnia, right?

You can read *The Lion, the Witch and the Wardrobe* (1950) simply as a riveting adventure. But you can also notice the way C. S. Lewis uses Edmund's betrayal to parallel that of Judas, and Aslan's sacrifice to parallel that of Christ. And if you do, the story picks up added weight and meaning. Then *The Lion, the Witch and the Wardrobe* doesn't simply exist in a far-off fairy-tale world. Its story becomes timeless, speaking of the pain and grief and guilt and forgiveness and hope that human beings everywhere have always lived with. And that is a story that never grows old.

C. S. Lewis isn't the only writer who decided to create a character whose life looks a lot like Jesus's. (Although, as far as I know, he is the only one who made that character a lion.) A fictional character like Aslan, whose story parallels that of Jesus, is called a Christ figure. If you have your eye out for Christ figures in your reading, this list may be helpful.

1. crucified, wounds in the hands, feet, side, and head
2. in agony
3. self-sacrificing
4. good with children
5. good with loaves of bread, fishes, water, and wine

6. thirty-three years old when last seen
7. works as a carpenter
8. doesn't use fancy modes of transportation (feet or donkeys preferred)
9. believed to have walked on water
10. often seen with arms outstretched
11. spends time alone in the wilderness
12. tempted by the devil
13. last seen in the company of thieves
14. likes to tell stories and parables and uses wise sayings
15. carried his own cross
16. dead and buried, but came back to life on the third day
17. has disciples, twelve at first, although they are not all faithful to him
18. very forgiving
19. came to save an unworthy world

This list, of course, doesn't cover everything the Jesus of the Bible ever said or did. That's okay. It's not a list about religious belief; it's a list to help us recognize certain kinds of characters who we might come across in books.

Say we're reading a book, a novel. And let's say this novel has a man in it. The man is old, very poor, and his work is humble; he's not a carpenter but a *fisherman*. Jesus had some dealings with fishermen, too, so there's a point of connection. And the old fisherman hasn't had much good luck for a long time, so no one believes in him. But one young boy does. There're two points from our list: the old man is *good with children.* And *he has a disciple.*

And this old man is *very good and pure,* so that's another point of connection. Because the world that he lives in isn't quite so good. You could even think of it as fallen.

Out fishing by himself, the man hooks a big fish that takes him out far beyond where he's been before, to where the sea becomes a *wilderness.* He's all alone. He *suffers a lot of pain.* His *hands* are ripped up by struggling with the fishing line; he thinks he's broken something in his *side.* But he encourages himself with *wise sayings* like "A man is not made for defeat. A man can be destroyed but not defeated."

The man's struggles with the fish last *three days.* The people left on land think he is *dead.* His great fish is ruined by sharks, but he manages to drag its skeleton back to the port. When he returns, it's like he's *come back to life.* He has to walk up a hill from the water to his shack. He carries the mast of his ship, which makes him look like *a man carrying a cross.* Then he lies on his bed, exhausted. *His arms are thrown out to the sides. His hands, hurt and raw, are showing.*

And the next morning, when everyone sees the skeleton of the giant fish, even the doubters begin to believe in the old man again. He brings *a kind of hope* to his world.

And . . . yes? Did you have a question?

Didn't Ernest Hemingway write a book like that?

Yes, *The Old Man and the Sea* (1952). It's easy to spot that he meant the old man, Santiago, to be a Christ figure.

It's not always so simple. Not every Christ figure will have all nineteen items on our list. (Even Santiago didn't.) They don't have to be male. Don't have to be human—think of Aslan. Don't have to be Christian. Don't even have to be good. But if a character is a certain age, does certain things (hands out wine and bread, blesses children, you know what I mean), suffers in certain ways (keep an eye out for those wounds in the hands, feet, and/or side), or sacrifices himself or herself or itself for others (that's the big one), then you should pay attention.

Why are there Christ figures? The short answer is that the author wants to make a certain point. Perhaps the character's sacrifice will mean more to us if we see it as similar to the greatest sacrifice we know of. Maybe it has to do with saving somebody (or everybody). Or hope. Or miracles. But count on it, the writer is up to something. Noticing that he's using a character as a Christ figure is one way to start figuring it out.

CHAPTER EIGHT

Hanseldee and Greteldum

BY NOW I'VE beaten you severely about the head and shoulders with the idea that all literature grows out of other literature. That could include novels, stories, plays, poems, songs, opera, movies, television, commercials, and possibly a variety of electronic media we haven't even seen yet. So let's try being writers for a moment. You want to borrow from some source to add a bit of flesh to the bare bones of your story. Who ya gonna call?

Actually, *Ghostbusters* is not a bad answer. For right now, anyway. But will people in a hundred years know this movie? Maybe not.

Something a little more traditional? Homer? Half

of the people who read that name will think of the guy who says, "D'oh!" and not of the guy who wrote *The Iliad.* Shakespeare, then? He's been the go-to guy for four hundred years. But some people think quoting Shakespeare makes you look stuck up, or like you're trying too hard. Plus all the good quotes are already taken.

James Joyce? Too complex. T. S. Eliot? He's all quotes from other writers to begin with.

It's tough being a writer. What can you find to use that *all* of your readers will know?

Alice in Wonderland. Treasure Island. The Narnia novels. *The Cat in the Hat. Goodnight Moon.* We may not all know Shylock (he's from Shakespeare's *The Merchant of Venice,* by the way), but we all know Sam-I-Am. Fairy tales, too. "Snow White." "Sleeping Beauty."

So if you're a writer and you want to use a fairy tale, what do you do?

You might decide to tell the whole story, just as your readers know it, only more thoughtfully and deeply than a brief fairy tale can manage. So you expand it into a novel. Robin McKinley did this to "Beauty and the Beast" when she wrote *Beauty* (1978). Or you could shake things around, perhaps give us "Hansel and Gretel" from the point of view of the witch (who was living peacefully enough in her gingerbread cottage before two brats started nibbling on the window frames). Or Morgan le Fay's side of the King Arthur legend, as Marion Zimmer Bradley did with *The Mists of Avalon* (1982). Or you might change the time and the setting. Frances Hodgson Burnett took "Cinderella" into Victorian London and gave us *A Little Princess* (1905).

You, the writer, can pick and choose, deciding what you're going to keep of the old story and what you're going to let go. Frances Hodgson Burnett certainly did. She kept the good and lovely little girl (Sara doesn't think she's pretty, but other people do) whose mother is dead. She kept the mean stepmother—well, almost. Sara's father doesn't get married a second time, but he does send Sara to a boarding school, where Miss Minchin, the headmistress, is as cruel as any wicked stepmother right out of the Brothers Grimm. Once Sara's father dies and Sara is left penniless, Miss Minchin makes Sara slave in the kitchen, trudge out into stormy weather on errands, and sleep in a freezing attic full of rats. Burnett kept the stepsisters but changed them. Sara's two close friends at school are not wicked in the least, but they can't help Sara much without bringing Miss Minchin's wrath down on their heads. And they *are* spoiled, at least compared to Sara—they get enough to eat, warm clothes to wear, and an education. Sara gets none of these things.

Burnett didn't need the ball. She had no use for the glass slipper or for Prince Charming. But she kept the fairy godmother—again, with her own twist. A kind neighbor takes pity on Sara and sends her things—new clothes, warm blankets, delicious food, books to read—in such a secret and mysterious way that it seems like magic. In the end, it turns out that this kind neighbor is, in fact, Sara's guardian, a combination of a fairy godfather and a new father to make up for the one she lost. Sara goes to live a life of riches and luxury with him. A happy ending, just like every fairy tale should have.

Burnett used several pieces of the "Cinderella" story to create her novel. You, as the writer, don't have to. Maybe you only want the glass slipper, and it isn't even glass, it's a Nike running shoe. Maybe you just want a trail of bread crumbs, or a sleeper wakened by a kiss. You can bring the whole story to your reader's minds with just one small detail.

Why? Because fairy tales and legends, like Shakespeare and the Bible, and all other writing and telling, belong to the one big story. And also because, since we were old enough to be read to or to be propped up in front of a television, we've been living on that story.

As readers, we want something new in our stories, but we want familiarity too. We want a new novel to be not quite like anything we've read before. At the same time, we want it to be enough like stories we already know that we can use those stories to make sense of it. If a book manages both things at once, newness and familiarity, it creates a harmony—a new tune that sings along with the melody of the main story. And those harmonies are where a sense of depth comes from. Those harmonies may come from the Bible, or from Shakespeare, or from humbler, more familiar stories.

So the next time you go to the bookstore and carry home a new novel, don't forget your Brothers Grimm.

CHAPTER NINE

It's Greek to Me

In these last three chapters we've talked about three sorts of myths: Shakespearean, biblical, and folk or fairy tales. The connection between the Bible (or religion in general) and myth sometimes causes trouble. If you take "myth" to mean "untrue," you're going to be upset if somebody calls any part of religion a myth. But that's not what I mean by "myth."

When I say "myth," I mean something that helps explain us to ourselves in ways that physics, philosophy, mathematics, chemistry, can't. That explanation takes the form of stories that are a part of our group memory, things that everybody knows. These stories shape our culture, the way we live. And, in turn, the stories are shaped and changed by the lives we lead. They become a way of seeing the world and seeing ourselves.

Let's say it this way: **myth is a body of story that matters.**

Every community has its own body of story that matters. In European and European-American cultures, of course, there's a source for myth that almost everyone will recognize. When most of us think of myth, we think of Greece and Rome.

You don't believe me? In the town where I live, the sports teams at the college are the Spartans. Our high school teams are the Trojans. In my state we have a Troy, an Ithaca, a Sparta, a Romulus, a Remus, and a Rome. Now, if a town in the middle of Michigan can be called Ithaca, it suggests that Greek myths have some pretty good staying power.

Rick Riordan certainly thought so when he made his hero the son of a Greek god. Wading into *The Lightning Thief* (2005), you'll run into not just Percy's dad, Poseidon, but Zeus and Athena and Hades and the whole crowd on Mount Olympus. You'll also find more than a bit of Greek myth hiding inside J. K. Rowling's *Harry Potter and the Sorcerer's Stone* (1998). What guards the entrance to the place where the stone has been hidden? That's right, a three-headed dog. Any other three-headed dogs you know of? If you've read any Greek myths, you might remember that the underworld is guarded by a three-headed dog named Cerberus. Only one living person ever got past Cerberus. His name was Orpheus, and he was the greatest musician of his time.

He soothed Cerberus to sleep with his lyre (that's a bit like a harp, if you're interested) and went on to rescue his beloved, Eurydice, from the land of the dead. Or he tried to. Things didn't quite go as planned. But his story was there for J. K. Rowling when Harry and his friends needed to get past Fluffy.

Other myths stay in our minds as well. Like Icarus. I'm always a bit surprised, though, that Icarus gets all the attention. It was his father, Daedalus, who built the wings. The myth tells how Daedalus and Icarus have been imprisoned in a giant maze, the Labyrinth (which, ironically, Daedalus himself built). They know there is no way to escape by land or sea, so Daedalus builds, for himself and his son, two sets of wings made of reeds and wax. Daedalus flies safely to the mainland, but Icarus is too thrilled at the feel of flight to listen to his father's warnings. He flies higher . . . and higher . . . and higher . . . until the sun melts the wax in his wings. He falls, drowning in the sea.

The fall of Icarus remains deeply fascinating for us. We can see so much in it. There's the attempt of a parent to save a child and the grief of having failed. The solution that is as deadly as (or worse than) the problem it was trying to fix. The passion and enthusiasm that leads to self-destruction. The clash between the sober wisdom of adulthood and the recklessness of youth. And the terror involved in that headlong fall to the sea. It's a story that is so deeply part of our thinking that it comes to the reader's mind unbidden whenever somebody in a book flies or falls.

In 1558, Pieter Brueghel painted a wonderful picture, *Landscape with the Fall of Icarus.* Right at the front of the picture we can see a plowman with his ox. Just beyond him is a shepherd and his flock. At sea, a merchant ship sails calmly along. This is a scene of everyday activity. Everything is calm and ordinary. Except in the lower right corner of the painting, where you can see a pair of legs just about to disappear into the water.

That's our boy.

He really doesn't have much of a presence in the picture, but he still makes all the difference. Without those legs, without the sense of sadness and pity and helplessness they bring to the viewer, this is just a picture of farming and sailing without much to say for itself.

There are two great poems based on this piece of art. One is W. H. Auden's "Musée des Beaux Arts" (1940) and the other is William Carlos Williams's "Landscape with the Fall of Icarus" (1960). They're wonderful poems, each different from the other in tone, style, and form. But each has something to say about how the world goes on even in the face of our private tragedies.

Williams's poem talks about the visual elements of the painting, trying to capture the scene while sneaking in something about the theme. Even the way the poem looks on the page, tall and narrow, makes a reader think of the body plummeting from the sky.

> According to Brueghel
> when Icarus fell
> it was spring
>
> a farmer was ploughing
> his field
> the whole pageantry
>
> of the year was
> awake tingling
> near
>
> the edge of the sea
> concerned
> with itself
>
> sweating in the sun
> that melted
> the wings' wax
>
> unsignificantly
> off the coast
> there was

a splash quite unnoticed
this was
Icarus drowning

Auden's poem, on the other hand, is a meditation on what suffering is, and why the outside world takes no interest in our private disasters.

About suffering they were never wrong,
The Old Masters: how well they understood
Its human position; how it takes place
While someone else is eating or opening a window
    or just walking dully along . . .

It is astonishing and pleasing that the same painting can bring forth these two very different responses. Still, it all goes back to the myth: the boy, the wings, the unscheduled dive.

Greek and Roman myths, of course, are much more than Icarus. There are stories of doomed and desperate families (Oedipus, anyone?), bold searchers after treasure (Jason and the Argonauts), wronged women violent in their grief and madness. (Would you like Aeneas and Dido, or Jason and Medea?) There are stories of heroes, many of them the sons and daughters of gods. But these heroes did not always act in ways that are particularly divine.

Take *The Iliad*. Many people assume that *The Iliad*

is the story of the Trojan War, the war between the Greeks and the Trojans. It's not, though. It's the story of the wrath of Achilles. In other words, the story of how Achilles got really mad, and what happened afterward.

Achilles becomes angry with his leader, Agamemnon, and decides to sit out the war. He refuses to fight until his best friend is killed by the Trojans. At this point he turns his anger against the Trojans' greatest hero, Hector. In the end Achilles kills Hector and the Greeks win the war.

Oh, the reason Achilles got so mad? Agamemnon took away his war prize, something Achilles himself had stolen from the Trojans. Pretty trivial, right? It gets worse. The prize is a woman. What Agamemnon takes away from Achilles is his slave, the woman he kidnapped.

Is that noble? Hardly. And yet, somehow, this story has come to stand for ideals of heroism and loyalty, sacrifice and loss.

Later, in *The Odyssey*, Homer gave us the trials and struggles of another hero, Odysseus, as he tries to make his way home from the Trojan War. It's not easy; it takes him ten years. And his wife, Penelope, waits for him all that time.

Other writers don't always have their characters sulking when their kidnapped women are taken away from them, fighting bloody duels on the battlefield, or waiting a decade for their husbands to show up. But they *do* often show characters acting out of the same needs, desires, and patterns. The need to protect one's family: Hector. The need to maintain one's dignity: Achilles. The fight to return home: Odysseus. The determination to remain faithful and to keep hope alive: Penelope.

In two stories about legendary heroes behaving in very human ways, Homer gives us the four great struggles of the human being. No wonder so many writers have often borrowed from and imitated Homer and the other tales of Greek and Roman mythology.

Writers and readers share knowledge of these stories, this mythology. So when writers use it, we recognize it. Sometimes we understand exactly what the writer meant. Sometimes we only get a hint. Still, that recognition makes our experience of literature richer, deeper, more meaningful, so our own modern stories also matter. They also share in the power of myth.

CHAPTER TEN

It's More Than Just Rain or Snow or Springtime

IT WAS A dark and stormy might.

What, you've heard that one? Right, Snoopy. And Charles Schulz had Snoopy write it because it was a cliché. It had been one for a very long time back when your favorite beagle decided to become a writer. Edward Bulwer-Lytton, a famous Victorian novelist, actually did begin a (bad) novel with "It was a dark and stormy night." And now you know everything you need to know about dark and stormy nights. Except for one thing.

Why?

You wondered that too, didn't you? Why would a

writer want the wind howling and the rain pouring down?

You may say that every story needs a setting and that weather is part of the setting. That is true, by the way, but it isn't the whole deal. There's much more to it. Here's what I think: weather is never just weather. **It's never just rain.** And that goes for snow, sun, warmth, cold, and sleet too.

But let's think about rain for a moment.

Rain can be a plot device; it can make the characters seek shelter, get stranded or lost or stuck somewhere, waiting for it to end. This can be very handy for an author. Rain can also bring along tons of atmosphere. It's more mysterious, murkier, more isolating than most other weather conditions. (Fog is good too, of course.) Then there is the misery factor. Rain can make you more wretched than anything else you'll meet in the outside world. With a little rain and a bit of wind, you can die of hypothermia on the Fourth of July. And there's also something democratic about it. Rain falls on *everybody*. You can be rich or poor, guilty or innocent, male or female, young or old, powerful or weak, and it doesn't matter. Everybody gets wet.

What else can rain do? For one thing, it's clean. So if you want a character to be cleansed, let him walk through the rain to get somewhere. He can be quite transformed when he gets there. (He might also have a cold, but that's another matter.) He can be less angry, less confused, more sorry—whatever you want.

Rain can also bring new life and hope. This is partly because we associate it with spring. (April showers do in fact bring May flowers.) But also think of the story of Noah. Lots of rain, major flood, ark, cubits, dove, olive branch, rainbow. This flood is the big eraser. It destroys life on earth but also allows a brand-new start. Rain can bring the world back to life.

So an author can use rain to do just about anything he or she wants. Other kinds of weather, too. Fog is good. It almost always means some kind of confusion. Authors use fog to suggest that people can't see clearly. Charles Dickens starts out *A Christmas Carol* with fog filling the streets of London—a good setting for Ebenezer Scrooge, who has lost his way and needs ghostly help to find it again.

Snow? It can mean as much as rain. Snow is clean, plain, warm (if it covers you like a blanket), threatening, inviting, playful, suffocating. You can do just about anything you want with snow.

But an author doesn't have a quick shower of rain, or a flurry or snow, or a flood or a blizzard, for no reason at all. Like I said, it's never just rain.

And it never just happens to be spring, or fall, or winter, either.

Here's my favorite snippet of poetry:

That time of year thou mayst in me behold
When yellow leaves, or none, or few, do hang

Upon those boughs which shake against the cold:
Bare ruined choirs, where late the sweet birds sang.

(Oh, sorry, you need a translation? Try this: "If you look at me, you'll see a particular season. It's the season when only a few yellow leaves, or maybe none at all, are hanging on branches that are shaking in the wind, as if they're cold. Those branches are like bare and ruined balconies for choirs where, a while ago, sweet birds used to sing." But it sounds a lot better the way Shakespeare says it.)

That's Shakespeare's Sonnet 73. I like it for a lot of reasons. But the thing that really works here is the meaning. The speaker of the poem is seriously feeling his age, and making us feel it too. He's talking about getting old, and he's talking about a particular season: fall. November in the bones. It makes my joints ache just to think about it.

Now to the nuts and bolts. Shakespeare didn't invent this metaphor. Fall = middle age was a cliché long before he got hold of it. What he does is *use* this old metaphor in a new way, getting so specific and detailed (yellow leaves, branches shivering in the wind, missing birds) that it forces us to really *see* two things. One is what he's actually describing: the end of autumn and the coming of winter. The other is the thing he's really talking about: standing on the edge of old age.

For as long as anyone's been writing, the seasons

have stood for the same set of meanings. Maybe it's written into our brains that spring has to do with childhood and youth. Summer is adulthood and romance and passion and satisfaction. Autumn is failing health, weakness, and middle age and tiredness (but also harvest, which makes us think of eating our fill and having lots stored up for the winter). And then winter is old age and resentment and death.

Writers know that this is how we naturally think about the seasons, and they make use of that. When Shakespeare asks his beloved, "Shall I compare thee to a summer's day?" we know without thinking about it that this is much more flattering than if he'd compared her to, say, January eleventh. The White Witch doesn't make it eternal spring in Narnia, does she? The idea is practically funny. She makes it always winter (and never Christmas) because, well, she's evil, and so she hates the very idea of new life, new growth, happiness, and forgiveness. It takes Aslan to bring all of those things. And, of course, the spring.

Or take Henry James. He wants to write a story in which America (youth, enthusiasm) comes into contact with Europe (stuffy, dull, bound by rules and traditions). So he comes up with a girl, American, young, fresh, direct, open, naive, and something of a flirt. And he comes up with a man, also American but who's lived for a long time in Europe. The man is slightly older, bored, worldly, shut off to his emotions. She's all spring and sunshine; he's all frosty stiffness. Names, you ask? *Daisy* Miller and Frederick *Winterbourne*. Really, it's just too perfect. Once you notice the names, you pretty much know things will end badly, since daisies can't survive in winter. And end badly they do.

Every writer can use the seasons, and every writer does so in a slightly different way. What readers learn, finally, is that it's not simple. We can't assume that "summer" means X and "fall" means Y. But writers know there's a set of patterns that can be used in different ways. Sometimes a writers uses the patterns straight, and winter means what we expect it to mean—cold, death. Sometimes a writer turns our expectations around, and summer isn't warm and rich and happy; instead it's dusty and hot and miserable. The patterns are still the same, though, no matter how the writer uses them. And they've been around for a very long time.

So when you open up a book, check the weather, and the calendar too. If it's raining or snowing, if it's winter or summer, if the characters are shivering or sweating—it all matters.

CHAPTER ELEVEN

Is That a Symbol?

SURE IT IS.

That's one of the most common questions in class, and that's the answer I usually give. *Is that a symbol?* Sure, why not?

It's the next question where things get tricky. *What does it mean, what does it stand for?* I often come back with something clever, like "Well, what do you think?" Everybody thinks I'm making a joke or not doing my job, but neither one is true. Seriously, what do *you* think it stands for? Because that's probably what it does stand for. At least for you.

Here's the problem with symbols: people expect them to mean something. Not just any something, but one something in particular. Just one meaning. No more. You know what? It doesn't work like that.

Oh, sure, there are some symbols that work in a pretty simple manner. A white flag means "I give up, don't shoot!" So some symbols *do* have just one meaning. But most don't. Most have a range, a lot of different possible meanings.

Let's think about rivers.

In *Adventures of Huckleberry Finn* (1885), Mark Twain sends Huck and the escaped slave Jim down the Mississippi on a raft. The river is a little bit of everything in the novel. At the beginning it floods, killing animals and people. So is the river a symbol of destruction and danger? But Jim is using the river to escape from slavery. So is the river—which flows freely, even overflows its banks—a symbol of freedom? But the river is carrying Jim and Huck south, deeper into slave territory. So does the river stand for slavery? Oppression? A fate you can't get away from?

The river is both danger and safety. It keeps Huck and Jim away from the people chasing them, and it also threatens to kill them. It also offers a place where Huck, a white boy, can get to know Jim, a black man, not as a slave but as a human being. And of course the river is really a road, and the journey is really a quest (remember, all trips are quests!) that allows Huck to grow up and make important choices about himself and his life.

The only thing we can be sure about this river is that it means *something*. But it may mean something different for every reader. We tend to give writers all the credit, but reading is also an event of the imagination. The creativity of the reader meets that of the writer, and in that meeting we puzzle out what he means, or what we understand he means.

And so each reader's experience of *Huckleberry Finn* is different, because each reader is different. We all bring different things to each book—what we've read before, what we think about and care about, who we are. So each reader must decide for himself or herself what the river means, and each one will be right.

So what does the river actually stand for? What do *you* think?

CHAPTER TWELVE

It's All Political

NOWADAYS WE THINK of *A Christmas Carol* as a nice holiday story about a bad man becoming good. But in 1843, when Charles Dickens wrote it, he was attacking a common political belief: that it was wrong to give food to the poor, or to find ways to produce more food so that people would not go hungry. This kind of help would only encourage poor people to have more children who would be poor themselves. Helping poor people would just make more poor people.

Scrooge actually says so. He wants nothing to do with the cold, hungry people all around him, and if they would rather starve than go to a workhouse or a debtor's prison (the only places they would likely be given any food at all), then, by golly, "they had better do it, and decrease the surplus population."

Did you get that? "Decrease the surplus population"? He means they should die (quickly, too!) so that there won't be as many poor people in the world. What a guy!

If nasty old Scrooge were just a single, selfish man, if he were the only man in England who needed to learn the lesson that the poor are people too, the story would not mean as much as it does. No, Dickens doesn't pick Scrooge because he's unique. He picks him because Scrooge shows us the way many people of his time talked and felt. Because there is something of Scrooge in us and in society.

We can have no doubt that the story is meant to change us, and by changing us, to change the world. Dickens is a social critic, which means he's using his stories to point out things he doesn't like about the society he lives in. He's a sneaky one, too. He's always so entertaining that we might not notice that he's using *A Christmas Carol* to tell us that there's a wrong way to think about the poor, and a right way too. But that's what he's doing.

Nearly all writing is political on one level or another. That doesn't mean it has to be about elections, or political parties, or that it has to try to make you vote one way or the other. (In fact, writing that tries to do that usually ends up being preachy, too simple, and dull.) What I mean by "political" is writing that thinks about human problems, about how human beings in groups get along, about the rights individuals possess (or should), and about the wrongs committed by those in power.

You may not think of the stories of Edgar Allan Poe as political. Mostly it seems like he's just out to give his readers a good scare. And he does. But some of his tales deal with a part of society most of us just get to read about: the nobility. Dukes and duchesses, earls and countesses, princes and princesses.

In "The Masque of the Red Death" (1842), there's a terrible plague that is killing people left and right. In the middle of all that suffering, a prince throws a party. All of his friends come, and the prince locks the doors, shutting out all the sick people beyond the walls. But the plague finds its way in somehow, and in the morning all these rich people, leading their lives of luxury, are dead.

In "The Fall of the House of Usher" (1839), Roderick Usher and his sister, Madeline, are the last survivors of an old, aristocratic family. They live in a rotting mansion that is falling to pieces around them. They're in pretty bad shape themselves. Madeline is sick with a "wasting disease" and Roderick looks and acts much older than he is. Plus he seems a bit insane. When the brother and sister finally die in each other's arms, the narrator of the story escapes just before their ancient house falls down and crashes into a black lake.

Poe's got something on his mind, something to say about people who are rich and have fancy titles and family histories of power and privilege. (Hint: he's not a fan.) And that, my friends, is political.

Ready for another example? How about "Rip Van Winkle"? Tell me what you remember about the story.

Okay. Rip Van Winkle, who's lazy and not much of a worker, goes hunting. Actually, he's just escaping from his nagging wife. He meets some odd characters playing ninepins, which is kind of like bowling, and he drinks a bit with them and falls asleep. When he wakes up, his dog is gone and his gun has rusted and fallen apart. He has white hair and a beard a mile long and very stiff joints. He makes his way back to town and finds out he's been asleep for twenty years and his wife is dead and everything has changed, including the signs at the hotel. And that's pretty much the story.

Pretty much. Except that we need to think about two questions.

1. What does it mean that Rip's wife is dead?
2. How does that connect with the changes in the hotel's sign?

During the twenty years that Rip's been asleep, the American Revolution has happened. The picture of the British King George on the sign at the inn has been changed into that of George Washington. The flagpole has a new, American flag. And Rip's wife is dead.

To everybody else she was just Dame Van Winkle, but to Rip she was a bully, a tyrant, someone with unfair power over him. And now she's gone. Rip finds out that he's free, and he likes it.

So everything's better?

Definitely not. Liberty has brought some problems with it. Things have become a little run-down. The hotel has some broken windows, and the town and its people are generally a little more ragged than they were before the war. But there's a kind of energy that drives them. They know that their lives are their own, and nobody, by golly, is going to boss them around. They speak their minds and do what they want. In other words, this slightly scruffy bunch of people is on the way to figuring out for itself what it means to be American and free.

So is every book political?

I can't go that far. I do think, though, that most books have something to say about the time and the place they were written in, and they say it in ways that can be called political. Let's say this: writers tend to be men and women who are interested in the world around them. Many of the things in that world are political. Who holds power and how they got it and what they do with it. Who has money and how they got it and what they do with it. Issues of justice and rights. Men and women and how they get along. Racial and ethnic groups and what they say and think and do to and about each other. Those are the sorts of things that often find their way onto the page.

Sometimes it's obvious. Sometimes the author hides the message so cleverly that we may not think of it as political, but it is.

It always—or almost always—is.

CHAPTER THIRTEEN

Geography Matters

LET'S GO ON vacation.

You say okay and then ask your first question, which is . . . *Who's paying? Which month? Can we get time off from school?*

No. None of those.

Where?

That's the one. Mountains or beaches, cities or campgrounds, canoeing or sailing. You know you have to ask because if you don't, I might take you fishing on some little stream twenty-seven miles from a dirt road when what you really wanted was to head to the beach.

Writers have to ask that question, too. So we readers should think about it. In a sense, every story or poem is a vacation. And every writer has to ask, every time, "Where are we going?"

What does it mean to the novel that its landscape is high or low, steep or shallow, flat or uphill all the way? Why did this character die on a mountaintop, that one on the savanna? Why is this poem set on the prairie? What exactly does geography mean to a work of literature?

Would "everything" be too much?

Okay, not in every book, but often. In fact, more often than you think.

Any boy and any man could take a trip down any river. But Huck Finn and Jim could only make the story we know as *Adventures of Huckleberry Finn* by being on one particular river, the Mississippi, traveling through that particular landscape and those particular towns and cities at one particular moment in history. It matters that they are going south, not north, because Jim is running away in the worst possible direction. It matters when they reach the town of Cairo and the Ohio empties into the Mississippi. If Jim had gotten off the raft at Cairo, he'd be a free man. But when the raft slips past Cairo in the fog, Jim is stuck traveling downstream and into the heart of slave territory.

Geography mattered to Laura Ingalls Wilder too. She tells us so. Look at the titles of her books (1932–39): *Little House on the Prairie. Little House in the Big Woods. On the Banks of Plum Creek. By the Shores of Silver Lake.* Each time, she's describing how one particular family lives in one particular place. And that place is the frontier, the very edge of what Wilder thinks of as civilization. If the Ingalls family didn't live on that edge, Wilder probably wouldn't have written down their adventures. The places made the stories happen.

And that's geography?

Sure, what else?

I don't know. History?

So what's geography, then?

I usually think of hills, creeks, deserts, beaches. Stuff like that. Stuff that shows on a map.

Exactly. Hills, etc. Rivers, hills, valleys, glaciers, swamps, mountains, prairies, seas, islands, *people*. The geography in books is usually about people living in particular spaces. How much do the places we live in make us into the people we are? Who can say? Writers, that's who.

Geography in literature can tell us a lot about almost any part of the book. Theme? Sure. Symbol? No problem. Plot? Without a doubt.

In Edgar Allan Poe's "The Fall of the House of Usher," the narrator spends the opening pages describing the bleakest landscape you ever saw. It's "a singularly dreary tract of country" with some "white trunks of decayed trees" and "a black and lurid tarn"—a pond without a ripple. By the time we get through all that, we're ready for the "bleak walls" of the house, with its "vacant eye-like windows" and the crack zigzagging right down its front. We're nervous and dismayed by all this description even before anything has happened. And that's one thing geography can do for a story.

Geography can also help us see what's going on inside a character. Especially when that geography changes. As it does when Harry Potter boards the Hogwarts Express at Platform 9¾. When the train leaves London, there are fields and sheep out the windows. Then it's "woods, twisting rivers, and dark green hills." A bit later there are mountains and forests. What ideas does that give you? The city, or the suburbs, where Harry lives with his aunt and uncle, is the place of Muggles—boring, stuffy, and above all, *not magical.* Getting to Hogwarts means heading into the wilderness, where things are wild, free, exciting, often dangerous, and magical as well. The geography tells you what's going to happen to Harry long before he figures it out himself.

Or consider Mary Lennox of *The Secret Garden* (1911). Mary starts the book out in India. She doesn't like it there. It's hot, so hot that she feels sick and weak a lot of the time. She's bored and lonely. There are no other children around, and her parents can't be bothered with her. Her only companions are her Indian servants. They don't like her. (Why would they? She orders them around, slaps them, and calls them names.) She doesn't like them. In fact, she doesn't like herself, the person she is in India.

And then she comes to England. To one particular

part of England—Yorkshire. She doesn't like it there either, at first. But the fresh, cool air gives her energy and strength. Spending time outside gives her new things to think about, so she's not bored anymore. She even begins to make some friends. She becomes a better person—happier, kinder, someone she can actually like. But she could not have become this person in India. Geography changed who she was and who she could become.

So near or far, high or low, north or south, east or west, the places of poems and fiction really matter. It isn't just setting. Place brings us to ideas, to the minds and hearts of the characters, to what the author is trying to say. It's enough to make you read a map.

INTERLUDE

One Story

WE'VE SPENT QUITE a while thinking about particular jobs that are involved when you read. Looking for quests. Keeping on eye on the weather and the season. Watching out for stories from myth. And all these things matter, of course, but there's something more important going on here. And here it is:

There's only one story.

One story. Everywhere. Always. Wherever anyone puts pen to paper or hands to keyboard or quill to parchment. They all take from and give back to the same story.

What's it about?

That's probably the best question you'll ever ask, and I apologize for giving you a really lame answer: I don't know.

It's not about anything. It's about everything. It's not about something the way Harry Potter is *about* a young man with a scar and a destiny. It's about everything that anyone wants to write about. I suppose it's really about ourselves, about what it means to be human.

I mean, what else is there?

Do writers know this? Do they think about it?

1. Good heavens, no.
2. Absolutely, yes.
3. Let me try again.

On one level, anybody who writes anything knows that you can't be completely original. Think of it this way: can you use a word no one else has ever used? Only if you're William Shakespeare or James Joyce, and even then, most of the time they use the regular words all the rest of us know. Can you put those regular words together in a combination that nobody has ever used before? Maybe, but you can't really be too sure. It's the same way with stories. Somebody has always gotten there first.

This is not a terrible thing, though. Writers notice all the time that their characters resemble somebody—Pippi Longstocking, Long John Silver, La Belle Dame sans Merci. And they go with it. What happens then, if the writer is good, is not that their work seems boring because it's been told before. Actually, the work becomes more interesting because it connects to something older. It means more. It has more to say.

So that's one answer. But here's another. Writers have to practice a kind of amnesia when they sit down to write. A kind of forgetting. Consider trying to write a poem . . . with every poet in the world looking over your shoulder. That's a lot of hot breath on the back of your neck. So, amnesia. When the writer gets to work, she has to shut out the voices and write what she writes, say what she has to say.

But she's been reading poetry since she was six. Reads a couple of new books of poetry a week. All of that stays in her mind. The history of poetry never leaves her. Even if she's not thinking about it, it's there. And it will come out in her poem.

Anything you write is connected to other written things. It's sort of a World Wide Web of writing. The English-teacher word for this is "intertextuality," but you don't really have to remember that. Just think of it this way: everything's connected.

Imagine a movie Western. You're writing your first Western? Good for you. What's it about? A big showdown? *High Noon.* A gunslinger who retires? *Shane.* A lonely outpost during an uprising? *Fort Apache, She Wore a Yellow Ribbon*—the woods are full of 'em. Cattle drive? *Red River.*

No, wait. I wasn't thinking of any of them.

Doesn't matter. Your movie will. Here's the thing:

you can't avoid them. The movies you have seen were created by men and women who had seen others, and so on, until every movie connected with every other movie ever made. If you've seen Indiana Jones being dragged behind a truck by his whip, then you've been touched by *The Cisco Kid* (1931), even if you've never seen it.

Let's take the most basic element, the hero. Will your hero talk a lot or not? If not, then he's in the tradition of Gary Cooper and John Wayne and (later) Clint Eastwood. If he does speak, just talks his fool head right off, then he's like James Garner. Or maybe you have two, one talker and one silent type—*Butch Cassidy and the Sundance Kid* (1969). Your guy is going to have a certain number of words to say, and no matter what you decide, audiences are going to hear echoes of earlier films, whether you are thinking of those films or not. And that, my friends, is intertextuality.

The second English-teacher word we've got to think about is "archetype." Archetype is a five-dollar word for pattern, or for the idea that there was once, long ago, something on which a pattern is based. Some original. Some idea that started it all.

It's like this. Somewhere back in myth, something—some part of a story—comes into being. It works so well, for one reason or another, that it keeps hanging around. It could be anything: a quest, a form of sacrifice, flight and falling, a shared meal—anything.

Whatever it is, it calls to us, alarms us, inspires us. And makes us want to hear it again. Again and again and again.

You'd think that these elements, these archetypes, would get worn out. But they actually work the other way—they get stronger. Here is that *aha!* factor again. When we hear or see or read one of these archetypes again, we feel a little thrill of recognition and say a little satisfied "Aha!" And we get to do that pretty often, because writers keep using them over and over.

Don't bother looking for the story that started it all, though. You can't find the first quest story, or the first flight. It's too far back. Perhaps there never was a single, first version of whatever myth we mean. Let's just say that somewhere, back in the mists of time, certain stories got told and retold. And today we borrow certain figures from them, like someone who flies and falls, or the young person who must go on a long journey.

These stories are always with us. Always in us. We can use them, change them, add to them whenever we want. That one story that has been going on forever is all around us. Readers and writers, tellers and listeners—we understand one another because we all know this same swirl of story. We only have to reach out into the air and pluck a piece of it.

CHAPTER FOURTEEN

Marked for Greatness

QUASIMODO IS A hunchback. Mary Shelley's creation (not Victor Frankenstein, but his monster) is a man of parts—literally. Oedipus has damaged feet. All are characters who are famous for their shapes as well as their behavior. Their shapes tell us something about them or about other people in the story.

First, it's obvious—or it should be obvious—that in real life, when people have any physical mark or scar or disability, it means nothing about who they are inside. In real life, a limp is just a limp.

In literature, it's often something else. In books, a physical flaw—a scar, a limp, an amputation, a twisted spine, an ugly face—can be a symbol. It has to do with being different, really. Being different on the outside is almost always a metaphor for being different on the inside.

In folktales or fairy tales, the hero is often marked in some way. He may be scarred or lamed, or wounded or born with a short leg, but he has some mark that sets him apart. You don't believe me? How many stories do you know in which the hero is different from everybody else in some way? And how many times is that difference something that can be seen? Why does Harry Potter have a scar, where is it, how did he get it, and what does it look like?

Oedipus is one of those marked heroes. One of the most famous characters from Greek myths, he is marked from childhood (just like Harry Potter). His marking isn't on his face, though; it's on his feet. If you were Greek and going to see Sophocles's famous play *Oedipus Rex*, you'd know this even before you got to the theater, because Oedipus's name means "wounded foot."

Oedipus's feet are damaged from the thong that was put through his Achilles tendons when he was sent away, as a baby, to die in the wilderness. His parents were frightened of the terrible prophecy that had been told about their baby, the prediction that he would grow up to kill his father and marry his mother. So they sent a servant to leave the baby out in the wilderness where he would die. Just to be safe, they had his feet lashed together so that he couldn't crawl away. Oedipus survives, of course, and actually does grow up to kill his father and marry his mother. And in the end, his injured feet are part of the evidence that proves who he really is and what he has really done.

Oedipus's scars tell his story. Harry Potter's do also. Their marks don't only show us that these two heroes are not like anybody else; their marks also show us what has happened to them. Harry's scar is there because Voldemort killed his parents . . . and tried to do the same to him. Oedipus's feet are damaged because his parents tried to kill *him.* And it's these events that turn Harry and Oedipus into who they are. Neither one would have done what he did if he had not been scarred or marked in that particular way.

What about characters who aren't scarred or marked by events, but who are born (or built) in a way that catches our attention? What about Mary Shelley? Her monster is built out of spare parts from a graveyard. And he's built at a particular moment in history. The industrial revolution was starting up, and this new world was a threat to everything people had believed for centuries. New science (and a new faith in science) shook old ways of thinking and believing. The nameless monster Victor Frankenstein builds is frightening because he represents the things this science could produce: forbidden knowledge, the result of science without care, thought, or compassion. He *looks* deformed and monstrous because he *is* a terrifying warning of what this brand-new science can bring about if we're not careful with it.

So does a character who *looks* horrible always *act* horribly? Not necessarily. Sometimes it's the other way around. Quasimodo, in Victor Hugo's *The Hunchback of Notre Dame* (1831), was born ugly. His face is deformed; his back is twisted. They say he's the ugliest person in Paris. But this hideous outside hides a brave and generous soul. Hugo uses Quasimodo's ugliness to point out how much better, kinder, and gentler this monstrous-looking person is than the others around him. They *look* normal but act selfishly, cruelly, monstrously. Quasimodo *looks* like a monster but acts like a hero.

Are deformities and scars always meaningful? Perhaps not. Perhaps sometimes a scar is just a scar, an injured foot or a hunchback merely that. But more often a physical mark means that the author wants to call our attention to something about the character or something about the book. After all, it's easier to create characters without imperfections. You give a guy a limp in Chapter Two, he can't go sprinting after the train in Chapter Twenty-four. So if a writer brings up a physical problem or a disability or a scar, he probably means something by it.

CHAPTER FIFTEEN

He's Blind for a Reason, You Know

HERE'S THE SETUP. You have a man, someone people admire. He's smart, strong; he can get things done. (He might be a little too quick to get angry, though.) This man has a problem. He doesn't even know it, but he's committed the two most awful crimes a person can commit. He's so confused about who he is and what he's done that he actually promises to hunt down the person who committed these crimes. He doesn't have a clue that the person he's promised to hunt down is himself.

He calls in an expert for help, someone who can show him the truth. When this person arrives, he's blind. Can't see a thing in the world.

As it turns out, though, this expert is able to see the truth that our main character can't see, that our strong, smart, capable hero is the worst kind of criminal.

What did this fellow do?

Nothing much. Just kill his father and marry his mother.

We're back to Oedipus again. Tiresias is the blind seer who knows the whole truth about King Oedipus, but that truth is so horrible that Tiresias tries to hold it back. When he does blurt it out, it's in a moment of such anger that nobody believes him. Oedipus, meanwhile, can see perfectly well, except that he can't see a thing about what really matters. When he finally sees the true horror that is his life, he chooses to punish himself in a particularly horrible way.

He blinds himself.

THERE ARE A lot of things that have to happen when a writer introduces a blind character into a book or a play. There are many things that character can't do, or can only do with difficulty. Every move that character makes, everything that character says or everything other characters say about him or her, has to allow for that lack of sight. It's a lot of work for the author, so something important must be at stake when blindness pops up in a story. Clearly, the author wants to bring up other ways of seeing and not seeing—not just the physical.

Every now and then in this book, I feel I have to make something clear. This is one of those times. What I just said is absolutely true: when blindness, sight, darkness, and light are found in a story, it is nearly always the case that symbolic blindness and sight (who can understand things and who can't, who's paying attention and who's not) are at work.

Here's the thing: this is often true in books where nobody ever mentions sight or blindness.

So what's the point of putting in a blind character, or talking about blindness?

Good question. I think it's a matter of being subtle, or not. Writers can drop in vague hints about blindness, and some readers may notice but some will not. If writers want us—all of us—to notice something, they'd better put it out there where we can find it. It's hard to miss a blind character. So if one shows up, it's a fair bet that the author thinks blindness and sight are important.

In Theodore Taylor's *The Cay* (1969), a young boy, Phillip, who happens to be white, is shipwrecked on a cay, a small island, with Timothy, an elderly man who happens to be black. Phillip doesn't care for black people (an attitude taught to him by his mother). He's pretty disgusted to find that he's got to be living in close quarters with Timothy for who knows how long until they are rescued.

But the thing is, Phillip needs Timothy. He needs him because, when their ship was torpedoed by a Nazi submarine, Phillip was hurt. A blow on the head left him blind.

Now, Taylor could have had Phillip get injured a different way. A broken leg, say. That would still have meant that Phillip would be forced to depend on Timothy, and that would be the beginning of a relationship that would help Phillip leave his racism behind. But no. Phillip's blind. Which is perfect, because Phillip can't *see* Timothy or other black people as they truly are. Even when he has his sight, he can't do it. His heart and mind are blind as well as his eyes. When he learns to understand Timothy and to value the old man's courage, generosity, and strength, then Phillip is no longer blind.

Now back to Oedipus. Don't feel too bad. When we meet him again, in the play *Oedipus at Colonus*, it's many years later. Of course he's suffered greatly, but that suffering has made him whole again. Instead of being the world's worst criminal, he becomes a favorite of the gods, who welcome him into the next world with a miraculous death. He has reached a level of wisdom that he never had when he could see.

CHAPTER SIXTEEN

It's Never Just Heart Disease . . . and Rarely Just Illness

WHEN YOU GET sick, you're just sick. And you lie around in bed until you feel better. But in books, something else is going on when characters get sick. You should always notice what they're suffering from.

Take heart disease. In real life, heart disease is frightening, sudden, shattering, exhausting. But in books, it can be something else: poetic. It can be a symbol.

Aside from being the pump that keeps us alive, the heart is also seen as the place where the emotions come from. It has been for a long time. In both *The*

Iliad and *The Odyssey*, there are characters with "a heart of iron." (Iron being the newest and hardest metal anyone had discovered when Homer was alive.) It means tough-minded, determined, even a bit hard-hearted—in other words, just what we might mean by the same statements today. Dante, Shakespeare, Donne, Marvell, Hallmark . . . all the great writers talk about the heart when they talk about feelings.

Writers use it because we feel it. What shape are your valentine cards? When we fall in love, we feel it in our hearts. When we lose a love, we feel heartbroken. When we're overwhelmed by strong emotions, our hearts are full to bursting.

Everybody knows this. What, then, can a writer do with this knowledge? The writer can use heart disease as a kind of shorthand for the character. Someone can have any number of problems for which heart disease is a sign: a love affair gone wrong, loneliness, cruelty, disloyalty, cowardice, lack of determination. Or a bad heart can stand for something else—something about love in an imperfect world.

One of the most famous bad hearts in literature belongs to Beth March in Louisa May Alcott's *Little Women* (1868–1869). Now, Beth isn't a coward, or lonely, or cruel—of course she's not. We all know she's not. Beth is loving, gentle, peaceful, a bit shy, and pretty much perfect. She's so perfect that, when neither of her older sisters can be bothered to go and visit a poor family whose children are sick, Beth goes by herself. And she catches scarlet fever.

That's bad enough, and there are lots of very sad scenes where Beth is ill and nearly dies. But then she finally gets better—only not entirely. She's weak and never gets back her former strength. It may seem poetic, the way Beth fades away, but it's also quite realistic. Scarlet fever can damage the heart, and that's what happens to Beth. Finally her weakened heart just can't beat anymore, and Beth dies quietly, peacefully, perfectly. Her heart was broken—actually broken—because she loved too much.

Beth's bad heart doesn't stand for a sin or a flaw in herself. But it does make a point about her sisters, who are too selfish at heart to go and visit the family where Beth catches the disease. And beyond her sisters and her family, doesn't Beth's heart say something about the world around her? A heart that loves like Beth's will be damaged. A heart like Beth's is only fit for heaven. The rest of us, with our hearts full of selfishness and laziness and the other flaws that come with being ordinary humans, will just have to struggle on without her.

It's not only our hearts that can get sick, of course. There are plenty of other illnesses out there, and writers can make full use of them—particularly those writers who did their work in the days when illness was still mysterious. Folks began to understand the idea of germs in the 1800s, but even then, they could not do much about them. People got sick and died. Nobody was quite sure why. Since illness is so much a part of life, it was a part of literature also.

There are certain principles governing the use of disease in literary works. *Not all diseases are created equal.* Before modern plumbing, cholera (which you can catch by drinking dirty water) was nearly as common as, and even more deadly than, tuberculosis. But cholera rarely shows up in books. Tuberculosis does, all the time. Why? Image, mostly. Cholera has a bad reputation. It's ugly, horrible, smelly, and violent. Nobody is going to want to read about that malady.

What, then, makes a prime literary disease?

1. *It should be picturesque.* What, you don't think illness can be picturesque? Consider tuberculosis, which the nineteenth century called "consumption." Of course it's awful when a person has a coughing fit that sounds like he's trying to bring up a whole lung, but the sufferer with tuberculosis often takes on a sort of bizarre beauty. The skin becomes pale, the eye sockets dark. The patient looks like a martyr in a medieval painting.

2. *It should be mysterious in origin.* Again, consumption was a clear winner back in the nineteenth century. Today we know that tuberculosis is spread when someone has contact with infected blood, phlegm, or saliva for a long period of time. But many authors didn't know what we know today. The awful disease sometimes swept through whole families, but nobody was quite clear on how or why. Certainly John Keats had no idea that caring for his brother Tom, who was sick with tuberculosis, was pretty much sealing his own doom.

3. *It should have good possibilities for use as a symbol.* If there's a metaphor connected with smallpox, I don't want to know about it. Tuberculosis, on the other hand, was a *wasting disease.* A person who caught it wasted away, growing thinner and thinner. It was a perfect symbol for lives that were wasted, often lives of young people, lives that had just gotten started.

So characters in books drop like flies from tuberculosis. Often the disease is not even named. Sometimes a character is "delicate," "fragile," "sensitive," or "wasting away." Sometimes they "suffer from lung disease." Or maybe it's just a cough that won't go away, or times of weakness. A mere symptom or two would be enough for the audience the author was writing for. They were all too familiar with the disease.

Of course, tuberculosis isn't the only illness available for a writer who wants to make a point. When Henry James has had enough of Daisy Miller and decides to kill her off, he gives her Roman fever, an old name for malaria. Malaria works great, metaphorically. It actually means "bad air." People thought you got it from breathing harmful vapors in the hot, moist night. (They had no idea that the problem actually was the mosquitoes that were biting them on those hot nights.) Daisy suffers from symbolic "bad air" throughout her time in Rome—nasty gossip, harsh opinions, cold disapproval from the people she longs to impress. So malaria is perfect for her end.

Still, the old name, the one James actually uses, works even better. Daisy does indeed suffer from Roman fever. She's in an overheated, frantic state of eagerness to join the snobby upper class. ("We're dying to be exclusive," she says early on.) When she makes her fatal midnight trip to the Colosseum and is ignored by Winterbourne, she says, "He cuts me dead." And the next thing we know, she *is* dead. Roman fever perfectly captures what happens to Daisy, this fresh young thing from the wilds of America (Schenectady, actually). She's killed by the clash between her own lively youth and the rotten atmosphere of Europe, the Old World.

Wait. I thought Winterbourne was a vampire who sucked the life out of Daisy?

Sure. And he's the force of winter, too—coldness, bitterness, death. And he kills Daisy with Roman fever on top of all that. No writer, especially not one as good as Henry James, has to stick to one symbol or one metaphor. It all works together (and none of it works out well for Daisy).

Sometimes a character doesn't actually have to be sick. He can just *think* he's sick. When Mary Lennox of *The Secret Garden* meets her cousin, Colin, the boy spends all his time in bed, weak and miserable and sorry for himself, making everybody around him miserable too. He tells Mary he believes that he's going to die.

Mary, who is about as selfish and unhappy as Colin, doesn't have an ounce of sympathy for him. "I don't believe it!" she snaps. "You just say that to make people sorry. I believe you're proud of it. I don't believe it! If you were a nice boy it might be true—but you're too nasty!"

In fact, Mary is right. Colin isn't actually sick. But on another level, Colin is right. He *is* sick—sick of himself, sick of being entirely alone. He has no friends. His mother is dead. His father cannot bear to talk to him. His only companions are servants who hate him for his whining and bullying and tantrums. He is so alone, so cut off from anyone who cares about him, that it might actually kill him.

When Colin makes friends with Mary, and when Mary introduces him to her new friend Dickon, he starts to get better. When he gets outside into the secret garden with his new friends, he grows even stronger.

Colin's "sickness" wasn't real. But as a metaphor, it was very real. Trapped inside his room and inside himself, with nothing but his own misery and fear for company, Colin quite naturally becomes ill. When he gets outside his room (into the garden) and outside himself (by making friends), he's healthy for the first time in his life.

So when a character gets sick or dies, pay attention. What disease does she have, exactly? How did she get it? What would make her better—if anything can? A character in a book doesn't just keel over for no reason. Whatever makes him sick on the outside is likely to reveal something about him on the inside—if you look closely enough.

CHAPTER SEVENTEEN

Don't Read with Your Eyes

In *The Secret Garden*, Mary makes friends, sort of, with her maid, Martha. It's Martha's cheerful chatter and stories of life with her family that first help Mary become interested in something outside herself. And that sets her on a journey that will lead her to becoming a happy, healthy child.

Well, nice for Mary. But what about Martha? What about her many brothers and sisters, who live in a tiny cottage with not enough to eat? Are we worried about them?

You can worry if you want to. But Mary doesn't. Not even Martha does. Martha's quite matter-of-fact about the idea that her brothers and sisters go hungry every now and then. She also doesn't grumble about lighting fires and cleaning the house and getting one day off a month, while Mary jumps rope and plays in the garden.

None of this probably bothered Frances Hodgson Burnett, either. It seemed reasonable to her for a maid to work while a child of a rich family plays. That's the way things were. She didn't mean to make Mary seem heartless or Martha seem stupid for not getting worked up about it.

We don't have to agree with Mary or Martha or Burnett. We can think that Martha (who's probably not that much older than Mary) *shouldn't* have to work so hard. We can think something should be done about those children in that tiny cottage without enough to eat. But we probably shouldn't decide that the characters who don't think that way are villains.

It seems to me that if we want to get the most out of our reading, we have to try to take the works as they were meant to be taken. This is what I usually say: don't read with *your* eyes.

What I really mean is, don't read only from your own fixed position in the year two thousand and some. Instead, try to find a place to read from that allows you to understand the moment in time when the story was written.

When Frances Hodgson Burnett wrote *The Secret Garden*, many people believed that the poor were poor and the rich were rich because that's the way

God planned it. Since it was God's plan, it couldn't be changed, so there was no point in getting all upset about it. That's the attitude that the characters in the book act out.

But more importantly, Burnett did not write *The Secret Garden* about the class differences between Mary and Martha. She wrote it about a sullen, selfish girl and a spoiled, miserable boy who have nothing in their lives to love. When they find friendship and a garden to care for, they find happiness and health together.

To notice that Mary has a better life than Martha is fine. To make that difference the most important thing in our reading would be to miss the point. That would mean we were reading the book with the wrong set of eyes.

And this is not such an old book. What about, say, *The Iliad*? All that violence. Blood sacrifices. Looting. Lots of gods. Concubines. Indeed, the very setup of the epic—Achilles throwing a fit because his slave has been taken away from him—can make it hard for a modern reader to feel any sympathy for him. And when he proves he's back on track by slaughtering every Trojan in sight, it strikes us as pretty vile. Homer's audience would not have felt that way—but we do.

So what can this great work teach readers who do not live in ancient Greece?

Plenty, if we're willing to read with the eyes of a Greek. A really, really old Greek.

Achilles destroys the thing he holds most dear, his lifelong friend, and dooms himself to an early death by allowing his pride to overrule his judgment. Even great men must learn to bend. Anger is unbecoming. One day our destiny will come for us, and even the gods can't stop it. There are a lot of useful lessons in *The Iliad,* but we'll miss most of them if we read it with twenty-first-century eyes.

Does that mean we have to think everything the characters do is perfectly okay? Absolutely not. I think we should frown on keeping slaves and slaughtering entire cities full of people. At the same time, though, we need to remember that the Greek people for whom Homer wrote did not feel that way. So if we want to understand *The Iliad* (and it is worth understanding), we have to accept that, for the characters, violence, slavery, and murderous revenge were actually just fine.

CHAPTER EIGHTEEN

Is He Serious? And Other Ironies

NOW HEAR THIS: irony trumps everything.

Consider roads. Journeys, quests, personal growth. But what if the road doesn't lead anywhere? Or if the traveler chooses not to take the road?

We know that roads (and oceans and rivers and train tracks) exist in literature only so that someone can travel on them. If you show us a pathway, you'd better put your hero on it.

But then there's Samuel Beckett. In his dramatic masterpiece *Waiting for Godot* (1953), he creates two tramps and plants them beside a road they never take. Every day they return to the same spot, hoping somebody named Godot will show up, but he never does.

They never get on the road. And the road never brings anything interesting their way.

Of course, we catch on pretty quickly, and we figure out that the road *does* exist for those two tramps to take. The fact that they never do shows us that they are not living the lives they are meant to live—or any lives at all, really. If we didn't expect them to get on that road, though, this wouldn't work. Then the two tramps would become nothing more than two guys stranded in bleak, lonely country. But that's not all that they are. They're two guys stranded in bleak, lonely country beside a way of escape that they never even try to take. And that makes all the difference.

Irony? Yes.

Irony is what happens when something in literature—a symbol like a road, say—doesn't work the way we expect. Irony is what happens when a writer plays on our expectations and turns them around. Sometimes it's funny. Sometimes it's sad. Sometimes it's both. But irony always means that what you think is going to happen doesn't.

Take rain. Of course we already know that rain can stand for a great many things. But then irony kicks in. If you read a scene where a baby is being born (think about it: new life coming into the world) during a rainstorm, the rain would lead you, without you even spending much time on it, to a chain of ideas: rain—birth—promise—fertility—new life and hope. What, those ideas don't always pop into your mind when rain starts falling in a book? If you begin to read like an English professor, they will.

At the end of Ernest Hemingway's *A Farewell to Arms* (1929), the hero, Frederic, walks out into the rain just after his lover, Catherine, has died giving birth to their baby. None of those expectations that we listed above are going to work here. In fact, we're going to run into the opposite ideas: rain—death—grief—hopelessness—despair.

The mother and child, rather than loving each other, kill each other. Frederic walks out into a winter rain, a rain that comes right after a false spring. There's nothing cleansing about that rain. It doesn't bring new life or new hope. That's what irony does—it takes our expectations and turns them upside down, makes them work against us. What should happen doesn't.

You can pretty much do this with anything. Here's an example: *The Graveyard Book.* Remember that little boy, toddling into a cemetery, embraced by a family of spooks and specters, watched over by a vampire? Get what's going on here? Neil Gaiman knows that we have certain associations, certain ideas, that come with graveyards. Death, for instance. Fear. Chills and shivers. Graveyards are supposed to be scary. Ghosts and vampires are supposed to be dangerous.

Only they're not. In this particular book, all the danger lies outside the graveyard, and all the safety is inside that graveyard fence. When a writer does this, though, the original meaning of the symbol doesn't just go away. (*Hey, graveyards are supposed to be scary!*) It hangs on in our minds, sort of like an echo, making us notice and pay attention to the new meaning that the writer has given the symbol. *(Wait, this graveyard is practically cozy!)*

It goes on and on. What happens when a plane crash strands a group of children on a desert island with no adults to care for them? If you've read William Golding's *Lord of the Flies* (1954), you know what happens—the boys turn on one another. Civilization is stripped away, and innocent human beings become vicious predators. The wild island is the perfect symbol for the wildness that Golding suggests is inside every human being, even the youngest and most innocent. Just waiting for a chance to get out.

But wait. Maybe you have a group of girls, not a group of boys. A group, actually, of contestants in a beauty contest. Maybe, instead of hunting one another down, the girls end up supporting and helping one another. Maybe the evening gowns and beauty products that the girls were using to compete become the tools that allow them to survive. Maybe vicious competition, savage attacks, backstabbing, and betrayal are things that happen *off* the island, during the beauty pageant itself.

If you have all that, then you have Libba Bray's

Beauty Queens (2011).

Civilization is stripped away from these girls too, just as it was taken away from William Golding's boys. Only this kind of civilization (the kind that comes in the form of lipstick, hair spray, high heels, and hair remover) turns out not to have been worth having. The island becomes a place where the girls can find their true selves—which means they find courage, compassion, friendship, and love instead of cruelty, violence, and murder.

That's irony. (It's also very funny.)

Nearly all writers use irony sometimes. It adds richness to the literary dish. It keeps us readers on our toes. Irony makes us dig through layers of possible meaning, thinking hard about what the writer wants to say.

We must remember: **irony trumps everything.** In other words, every chapter in this book goes out the window when irony comes in the door.

How do you know if a writer is using irony?

Listen.

CHAPTER NINETEEN

A Test Case

The Garden Party

by Katherine Mansfield

AND AFTER ALL the weather was ideal. They could not have had a more perfect day for a garden party if they had ordered it. Windless, warm, the sky without a cloud. Only the blue was veiled with a haze of light gold, as it is sometimes in early summer. The gardener had been up since dawn, mowing the lawns and sweeping them, until the grass and the dark flat rosettes where the daisy plants had been seemed to shine. As for the roses, you could not help feeling they understood that roses are the only flowers that impress people at garden parties; the only flowers that everybody is certain of knowing. Hundreds, yes, literally hundreds, had come out in a single night; the green bushes bowed down as though they had been visited by archangels.

Breakfast was not yet over before the men came to put up the marquee.

"Where do you want the marquee put, Mother?"

"My dear child, it's no use asking me. I'd determined to leave everything to you children this year. Forget I am your mother. Treat me as an honored guest."

But Meg could not possibly go and supervise the men. She had washed her hair before breakfast, and she sat drinking her coffee in a green turban, with a dark wet curl stamped on each cheek. Jose, the butterfly, always came down in a silk petticoat and a kimono jacket.

"You'll have to go, Laura; you're the artistic one."

Away Laura flew, still holding her piece of bread and butter. It's so delicious to have an excuse for eating out of doors, and besides, she loved having to arrange things; she always felt she could do it so much better than anybody else.

Four men in their shirtsleeves stood grouped together on the garden path. They carried staves covered with rolls of canvas, and they had big tool bags slung on their backs. They looked impressive. Laura wished now that she had not got the bread and butter, but there was nowhere to put it, and she couldn't possibly throw it away. She blushed and tried to look severe and even a little bit shortsighted as she came up to them.

"Good morning," she said, copying her mother's voice. But that sounded so fearfully affected that she was ashamed, and stammered like a little girl, "Oh—er—have you come—is it about the marquee?"

"That's right, miss," said the tallest of the men, a lanky, freckled fellow, and he shifted his tool bag, knocked back his straw hat, and smiled down at her. "That's about it."

His smile was so easy, so friendly, that Laura recovered. What nice eyes he had, small, but such a dark blue! And now she looked at the others, they were smiling too. "Cheer up, we won't bite," their smile seemed to say. How very nice workmen were! And what a beautiful morning! She mustn't mention the morning; she must be businesslike. The marquee.

"Well, what about the lily lawn? Would that do?"

And she pointed to the lily lawn with the hand that didn't hold the bread and butter. They turned, they stared in the direction. A little fat chap thrust out his under lip, and the tall fellow frowned.

"I don't fancy it," said he. "Not conspicuous enough. You see, with a thing like a marquee," and he turned to Laura in his easy way, "you want to put it somewhere where it'll give you a bang slap in the eye, if you follow me."

Laura's upbringing made her wonder for a moment

whether it was quite respectful for a workman to talk to her of bangs slap in the eye. But she did follow him.

"A corner of the tennis court," she suggested. "But the band's going to be in one corner."

"H'm, going to have a band, are you?" said another of the workmen. He was pale. He had a haggard look as his dark eyes scanned the tennis court. What was he thinking?

"Only a very small band," said Laura gently. Perhaps he wouldn't mind so much if the band was quite small. But the tall fellow interrupted.

"Look here, miss, that's the place. Against those trees. Over there. That'll do fine."

Against the karakas. Then the karaka trees would be hidden. And they were so lovely, with their broad, gleaming leaves, and their clusters of yellow fruit. They were like trees you imagined growing on a desert island, proud, solitary, lifting their leaves and fruits to the sun in a kind of silent splendor. Must they be hidden by a marquee?

They must. Already the men had shouldered their staves and were making for the place. Only the tall fellow was left. He bent down, pinched a sprig of lavender, put his thumb and forefinger to his nose and snuffed up the smell. When Laura saw that gesture she forgot all about the karakas in her wonder at him caring for things like that—caring for the smell of lavender. How many men that she knew would have done such a thing? Oh, how extraordinarily nice workmen were, she thought. Why couldn't she have workmen for her friends rather than the silly boys she danced with and who came to Sunday night supper? She would get on much better with men like these.

It's all the fault, she decided, as the tall fellow drew something on the back of an envelope, something that was to be looped up or left to hang, of these absurd class distinctions. Well, for her part, she didn't feel them. Not a bit, not an atom . . . And now there came the chock-chock of wooden hammers. Someone whistled, someone sang out, "Are you right there, matey?" Matey! The friendliness of it, the—the—Just to prove how happy she was, just to show the tall fellow how at home she felt, and how she despised stupid conventions, Laura took a big bite of her bread and butter as she stared at the little drawing. She felt just like a work girl.

"Laura, Laura, where are you? Telephone, Laura!" a voice cried from the house.

"Coming!" Away she skimmed, over the lawn, up the path, up the steps, across the veranda, and into the porch. In the hall her father and Laurie were brushing their hats, ready to go to the office.

"I say, Laura," said Laurie, very fast, "you might just give a squiz at my coat before this afternoon. See if it wants pressing."

"I will," she said. Suddenly she couldn't stop herself.

She ran at Laurie and gave him a small, quick squeeze. "Oh, I do love parties, don't you?" gasped Laura.

"Ra-ther," said Laurie's warm, boyish voice, and he squeezed his sister too, and gave her a gentle push. "Dash off to the telephone, old girl."

The telephone. "Yes, yes; oh, yes. Kitty? Good morning, dear. Come to lunch? Do, dear. Delighted, of course. It will only be a very scratch meal—just the sandwich crusts and broken meringue shells and what's left over. Yes, isn't it a perfect morning? Your white? Oh, I certainly should. One moment—hold the line. Mother's calling." And Laura sat back. "What, Mother? Can't hear."

Mrs. Sheridan's voice floated down the stairs. "Tell her to wear that sweet hat she had on last Sunday."

"Mother says you're to wear that sweet hat you had on last Sunday. Good. One o'clock. Bye-bye."

Laura put back the receiver, flung her arms over her head, took a deep breath, stretched and let them fall. "Huh," she sighed, and the moment after the sigh she sat up quickly. She was still, listening. All the doors in the house seemed to be open. The house was alive with soft, quick steps and running voices. The green baize door that led to the kitchen regions swung open and shut with a muffled thud. And now there came a long, chuckling, absurd sound. It was the heavy piano being moved on its stiff castors. But the air! If you stopped to notice, was the air always like this? Little faint winds were playing chase, in at the tops of the windows, out at the doors. And there were two tiny spots of sun, one on the inkpot, one on a silver photograph frame, playing too. Darling little spots. Especially the one on the inkpot lid. It was quite warm. A warm little silver star. She could have kissed it.

The front door bell pealed, and there sounded the rustle of Sadie's print skirt on the stairs. A man's voice murmured; Sadie answered, careless, "I'm sure I don't know. Wait. I'll ask Mrs. Sheridan."

"What is it, Sadie?" Laura came into the hall.

"It's the florist, Miss Laura."

It was, indeed. There, just inside the door, stood a wide, shallow tray full of pots of pink lilies. No other kind. Nothing but lilies—canna lilies, big pink flowers, wide open, radiant, almost frighteningly alive on bright crimson stems.

"O-oh, Sadie!" said Laura, and the sound was like a little moan. She crouched down as if to warm herself at that blaze of lilies; she felt they were in her fingers, on her lips, growing in her breast.

"It's some mistake," she said faintly. "Nobody ever ordered so many. Sadie, go and find Mother."

But at that moment Mrs. Sheridan joined them.

"It's quite right," she said calmly. "Yes, I ordered them. Aren't they lovely?" She pressed Laura's arm. "I was passing the shop yesterday, and I saw them in the window. And I suddenly thought for once in my life I shall have enough canna lilies. The garden party was just an excuse."

"But I thought you said you didn't mean to interfere," said Laura. Sadie had gone. The florist's man was still outside at his van. She put her arm round her mother's neck and gently, very gently, she bit her mother's ear.

"My darling child, you wouldn't like a logical mother, would you? Don't do that. Here's the man."

He carried more lilies still, another whole tray.

"Bank them up, just inside the door, on both sides of the porch, please," said Mrs. Sheridan. "Don't you agree, Laura?"

"Oh, I do, Mother."

In the drawing room Meg, Jose and good little Hans had at last succeeded in moving the piano.

"Now, if we put this chesterfield against the wall and move everything out of the room except the chairs, don't you think?"

"Quite."

"Hans, move those tables into the smoking room, and bring a sweeper to take these marks off the carpet and—one moment, Hans—" Jose loved giving orders to the servants, and they loved obeying her. She always made them feel they were taking part in some drama. "Tell Mother and Miss Laura to come here at once."

"Very good, Miss Jose."

She turned to Meg. "I want to hear what the piano sounds like, just in case I'm asked to sing this afternoon. Let's try over 'This Life Is Weary.'"

Pom Ta-ta-ta Tee-ta! The piano burst out so passionately that Jose's face changed. She clasped her hands. She looked mournfully and enigmatically at her mother and Laura as they came in.

"This Life is Wee-ary,
A Tear—a Sigh.
A Love that Chan-ges,
This Life is Wee-ary,
A Tear—a Sigh.
A Love that Chan-ges,
And then . . . Good-bye!"

But at the word "Good-bye," and although the piano sounded more desperate than ever, her face broke into a brilliant, dreadfully unsympathetic smile.

"Aren't I in good voice, Mummy?" She beamed.

"This Life is Wee-ary,
Hope comes to Die.
A Dream—a Wa-kening."

But now Sadie interrupted them. "What is it, Sadie?"

"If you please, ma'am, Cook says have you got the flags for the sandwiches?"

"The flags for the sandwiches, Sadie?" echoed Mrs. Sheridan dreamily. And the children knew by her face that she hadn't got them. "Let me see." And she said to Sadie firmly, "Tell Cook I'll let her have them in ten minutes."

Sadie went.

"Now, Laura," said her mother quickly, "come with me into the smoking room. I've got the names somewhere on the back of an envelope. You'll have to write them out for me. Meg, go upstairs this minute and take that wet thing off your head. Jose, run and finish dressing this instant. Do you hear me, children, or shall I have to tell your father when he comes home tonight? And—and, Jose, pacify Cook if you do go into the kitchen, will you? I'm terrified of her this morning."

The envelope was found at last behind the dining-room clock, though how it had got there Mrs. Sheridan could not imagine.

"One of you children must have stolen it out of my bag, because I remember vividly—cream cheese and lemon curd. Have you done that?"

"Yes."

"Egg and—" Mrs. Sheridan held the envelope away from her. "It looks like mice. It can't be mice, can it?"

"Olive, pet," said Laura, looking over her shoulder.

"Yes, of course, olive. What a horrible combination it sounds. Egg and olive."

They were finished at last, and Laura took them off to the kitchen. She found Jose there pacifying the cook, who did not look at all terrifying.

"I have never seen such exquisite sandwiches," said Jose's rapturous voice. "How many kinds did you say there were, Cook? Fifteen?"

"Fifteen, Miss Jose."

"Well, I congratulate you."

Cook swept up crusts with the long sandwich knife, and smiled broadly.

"Godber's has come," announced Sadie, issuing out of the pantry. She had seen the man pass the window.

That meant the cream puffs had come. Godber's was famous for their cream puffs. Nobody ever thought of making them at home.

"Bring them in and put them on the table, my girl," ordered Cook.

Sadie brought them in and went back to the door. Of course Laura and Jose were far too grown-up to really care about such things. All the same, they couldn't help agreeing that the puffs looked very attractive. Very. Cook began arranging them, shaking off the extra icing sugar.

"Don't they carry one back to all one's parties?" said Laura.

"I suppose they do," said practical Jose, who never

liked to be carried back. "They look beautifully light and feathery, I must say."

"Have one each, my dears," said Cook in her comfortable voice. "Yer ma won't know."

Oh, impossible, fancy cream puffs so soon after breakfast. The very idea made one shudder. All the same, two minutes later Jose and Laura were licking their fingers with that absorbed inward look that only comes from whipped cream.

"Let's go into the garden, out by the back way," suggested Laura. "I want to see how the men are getting on with the marquee. They're such awfully nice men."

But the back door was blocked by Cook, Sadie, Godber's man, and Hans.

Something had happened.

"Tuk-tuk-tuk," clucked Cook like an agitated hen. Sadie had her hand clapped to her cheek as though she had a toothache. Hans's face was screwed up in the effort to understand. Only Godber's man seemed to be enjoying himself; it was his story.

"What's the matter? What's happened?"

"There's been a horrible accident," said Cook. "A man killed."

"A man killed! Where? How? When?"

But Godber's man wasn't going to have his story snatched from under his very nose.

"Know those little cottages just below here, miss?" Know them? Of course she knew them. "Well, there's a young chap living there, name of Scott, a carter. His horse shied at a traction engine, corner of Hawke Street this morning, and he was thrown out on the back of his head. Killed."

"Dead!" Laura stared at Godber's man.

"Dead when they picked him up," said Godber's man with relish. "They were taking the body home as I come up here." And he said to the cook, "He's left a wife and five little ones."

"Jose, come here." Laura caught hold of her sister's sleeve and dragged her through the kitchen to the other side of the green baize door. There she paused and leaned against it. "Jose!" she said, horrified, "however are we going to stop everything?"

"Stop everything, Laura!" cried Jose in astonishment. "What do you mean?"

"Stop the garden party, of course." Why did Jose pretend?

But Jose was still more amazed. "Stop the garden party? My dear Laura, don't be so absurd. Of course we can't do anything of the kind. Nobody expects us to. Don't be so extravagant."

"But we can't possibly have a garden party with a man dead just outside the front gate."

That really was extravagant, for the little cottages were in a lane to themselves at the very bottom of a steep rise that led up to the house. A broad road ran between. True, they were far too near. They were the greatest possible eyesore, and they had no right to be in that neighborhood at all. They were little mean dwellings painted a chocolate brown. In the garden patches there was nothing but cabbage stalks, sick hens, and tomato cans. The very smoke coming out of their chimneys was poverty-stricken. Little rags and shreds of smoke, so unlike the great silvery plumes that uncurled from the Sheridans' chimneys. Washerwomen lived in the lane and sweeps and a cobbler, and a man whose house front was studded all over with minute birdcages. Children swarmed. When the Sheridans were little, they were forbidden to set foot there because of the revolting language and of what they might catch. But since they were grown up, Laura and Laurie on their prowls sometimes walked through. It was disgusting and sordid. They came out with a shudder. But still one must go everywhere; one must see everything. So through they went.

"And just think of what the band would sound like to that poor woman," said Laura.

"Oh, Laura!" Jose began to be seriously annoyed. "If you're going to stop a band playing every time someone has an accident, you'll lead a very strenuous life. I'm every bit as sorry about it as you. I feel just as sympathetic." Her eyes hardened. She looked at her sister just as she used to when they were little and fighting together. "You won't bring a drunken workman back to life by being sentimental," she said softly.

"Drunk! Who said he was drunk?" Laura turned furiously on Jose. She said, just as they had used to say on those occasions, "I'm going straight up to tell Mother."

"Do, dear," cooed Jose.

"Mother, can I come into your room?" Laura turned the big glass doorknob.

"Of course, child. Why, what's the matter? What's given you such a color?" And Mrs. Sheridan turned round from her dressing table. She was trying on a new hat.

"Mother, a man's been killed," began Laura.

"Not in the garden?" interrupted her mother.

"No, no!"

"Oh, what a fright you gave me!" Mrs. Sheridan sighed with relief, and took off the big hat and held it on her knees.

"But listen, Mother," said Laura. Breathless, half choking, she told the dreadful story. "Of course, we can't have our party, can we?" she pleaded. "The band and everybody arriving. They'd hear us, Mother; they're nearly neighbors!"

To Laura's astonishment her mother behaved just like Jose; it was harder to bear because she seemed amused. She refused to take Laura seriously.

"But, my dear child, use your common sense. It's only by accident we've heard of it. If someone had died there normally—and I can't understand how they keep alive in those pokey little holes—we should still be having our party, shouldn't we?"

Laura had to say "yes" to that, but she felt it was all wrong. She sat down on her mother's sofa and pinched the cushion frill.

"Mother, isn't it terribly heartless of us?" she asked.

"Darling!" Mrs. Sheridan got up and came over to her, carrying the hat. Before Laura could stop her she had popped it on. "My child!" said her mother, "the hat is yours. It's made for you. It's much too young for me. I have never seen you look such a picture. Look at yourself!" And she held up her hand mirror.

"But, Mother," Laura began again. She couldn't look at herself; she turned aside.

This time Mrs. Sheridan lost patience just as Jose had done.

"You are being very absurd, Laura," she said coldly. "People like that don't expect sacrifices from us. And it's not very sympathetic to spoil everybody's enjoyment as you're doing now."

"I don't understand," said Laura, and she walked quickly out of the room into her own bedroom. There, quite by chance, the first thing she saw was this charming girl in the mirror, in her black hat trimmed with gold daisies, and a long black velvet ribbon. Never had she imagined she could look like that. Is mother right? she thought. And now she hoped her mother was right. Am I being extravagant? Perhaps it was extravagant. Just for a moment she had another glimpse of that poor woman and those little children, and the body being carried into the house. But it all seemed blurred, unreal, like a picture in the newspaper. I'll remember it again after the party's over, she decided. And somehow that seemed quite the best plan. . . .

Lunch was over by half past one. By half past two they were all ready for the fray. The green-coated band had arrived and was established in a corner of the tennis court.

"My dear!" trilled Kitty Maitland. "Aren't they too like frogs for words? You ought to have arranged them round the pond with the conductor in the middle on a leaf."

Laurie arrived and hailed them on his way to dress. At the sight of him Laura remembered again. She wanted to tell him. If Laurie agreed with the others, then it was bound to be all right. And she followed him into the hall.

"Laurie!"

"Hallo!" He was halfway upstairs, but when he turned round and saw Laura he suddenly puffed out his cheeks and goggled his eyes at her. "My word, Laura! You do look stunning," said Laurie. "What an absolutely topping hat!"

Laura said faintly, "Is it?" and smiled up at Laurie and didn't tell him after all.

Soon after that people began coming in streams. The band struck up; the hired waiters ran from the house to the marquee. Wherever you looked there were couples strolling, bending to the flowers, greeting, moving on over the lawn. They were like bright birds that had alighted in the Sheridans' garden for this one afternoon, on their way to—where? Ah, what happiness it is to be with people who are all happy, to press hands, press cheeks, smile into eyes.

"Darling Laura, how well you look!"

"What a becoming hat, child!"

"Laura, you look quite Spanish. I've never seen you look so striking."

And Laura, glowing, answered softly, "Have you had tea? Won't you have an ice? The passion-fruit ices really are rather special." She ran to her father and begged him, "Daddy, can't the band have something to drink?"

And the perfect afternoon slowly ripened, slowly faded, slowly its petals closed.

"Never a more delightful garden party . . ." "The greatest success . . ." "Quite the most . . ."

Laura helped her mother with the good-byes. They stood side by side on the porch till it was all over.

"All over, thank heavens," said Mrs. Sheridan. "Round up the others, Laura. Let's go and have some fresh coffee. I'm exhausted. Yes, it's been very successful. But oh, these parties, these parties!" And they all of them sat down in the deserted marquee.

"Have a sandwich, Daddy dear. I wrote the flag."

"Thanks." Mr. Sheridan took a bite and the sandwich was gone. He took another. "I suppose you didn't hear of a beastly accident that happened today?" he said.

"My dear," said Mrs. Sheridan, holding up her hand, "we did. It nearly ruined the party. Laura insisted we should put it off."

"Oh, Mother!" Laura didn't want to be teased about it.

"It was a horrible affair, all the same," said Mr. Sheridan. "The chap was married too. Lived just below in the lane, and leaves a wife and half a dozen kiddies, so they say."

An awkward little silence fell. Mrs. Sheridan fidgeted with her cup. Really, it was very tactless of Father. . . .

Suddenly she looked up. There on the table were all those sandwiches, cakes, puffs, all uneaten, all going to be wasted. She had one of her brilliant ideas.

"I know," she said. "Let's make up a basket. Let's send that poor creature some of this perfectly good food. At any rate, it will be the greatest treat for the children. Don't you agree? And she's sure to have neighbors calling in and so on. What a point to have it all prepared. Laura!" She jumped up. "Get me that big basket out of the stairs cupboard."

"But, Mother, do you really think it's a good idea?" said Laura.

Again, how curious, she seemed to be different from them all. To take scraps from their party. Would the poor woman really like that?

"Of course! What's the matter with you today? An hour or two ago you were insisting on us being sympathetic, and now—"

Oh, well! Laura ran for the basket. It was filled, it was heaped by her mother.

"Take it yourself, darling," said she. "Run down just as you are. No, wait, take the arum lilies too. People of that class are so impressed by arum lilies."

"The stems will ruin her lace frock," said practical Jose.

So they would. Just in time. "Only the basket, then. And, Laura!"—her mother followed her out of the marquee—"don't on any account—"

"What, Mother?"

No, better not put such ideas into the child's head! "Nothing! Run along!"

It was just growing dusky as Laura shut their garden gates. A big dog ran by like a shadow. The road gleamed white, and down below in the hollow the little cottages were in deep shade. How quiet it seemed after the afternoon. Here she was going down the hill to somewhere where a man lay dead, and she couldn't realize it. Why couldn't she? She stopped a minute.

And it seemed to her that kisses, voices, tinkling spoons, laughter, the smell of crushed grass were somehow inside her. She had no room for anything else. How strange! She looked up at the pale sky, and all she thought was, "Yes, it was the most successful party."

Now the broad road was crossed. The lane began, smoky and dark. Women in shawls and men's tweed caps hurried by. Men hung over the palings; the children played in the doorways. A low hum came from the mean little cottages. In some of them there was a flicker of light, and a shadow, crablike, moved across the window. Laura bent her head and hurried on. She wished now she had put on a coat. How her frock shone! And the big hat with the velvet streamer—if only it was another hat! Were the people looking at her? They must be. It was a mistake to have come; she knew all along it was a mistake. Should she go back even now?

No, too late. This was the house. It must be. A dark knot of people stood outside. Beside the gate an old, old woman with a crutch sat in a chair, watching. She had her feet on a newspaper. The voices stopped as Laura drew near. The group parted. It was as though she was expected, as though they had known she was coming here.

Laura was terribly nervous. Tossing the velvet ribbon over her shoulder, she said to a woman standing by, "Is this Mrs. Scott's house?" and the woman, smiling queerly, said, "It is, my lass."

Oh, to be away from this! She actually said, "Help me, God," as she walked up the tiny path and knocked. To be away from those staring eyes, or to be covered up in anything, one of those women's shawls even. I'll just leave the basket and go, she decided. I shan't even wait for it to be emptied.

Then the door opened. A little woman in black showed in the gloom.

Laura said, "Are you Mrs. Scott?" But to her horror the woman answered, "Walk in, please, miss," and she was shut in the passage.

"No," said Laura, "I don't want to come in. I only want to leave this basket. Mother sent—"

The little woman in the gloomy passage seemed not to have heard her. "Step this way, please, miss," she said in an oily voice, and Laura followed her.

She found herself in a wretched little low kitchen, lighted by a smoky lamp. There was a woman sitting before the fire.

"Em," said the little creature who had let her in. "Em! It's a young lady." She turned to Laura. She said meaningly, "I'm 'er sister, miss. You'll excuse 'er, won't you?"

"Oh, but of course!" said Laura. "Please, please don't disturb her. I—I only want to leave—"

But at that moment the woman at the fire turned

round. Her face, puffed up, red, with swollen eyes and swollen lips, looked terrible. She seemed as though she couldn't understand why Laura was there. What did it mean? Why was this stranger standing in the kitchen with a basket? What was it all about? And the poor face puckered up again.

"All right, my dear," said the other. "I'll thenk the young lady."

And again she began, "You'll excuse her, miss, I'm sure," and her face, swollen too, tried an oily smile.

Laura only wanted to get out, to get away. She was back in the passage. The door opened. She walked straight through into the bedroom, where the dead man was lying.

"You'd like a look at 'im, wouldn't you?" said Em's sister, and she brushed past Laura over to the bed. "Don't be afraid, my lass"—and now her voice sounded fond and sly, and fondly she drew down the sheet—"'e looks a picture. There's nothing to show. Come along, my dear."

Laura came.

There lay a young man, fast asleep—sleeping so soundly, so deeply, that he was far, far away from them both. Oh, so remote, so peaceful. He was dreaming. Never wake him up again. His head was sunk in the pillow, his eyes were closed; they were blind under the closed eyelids. He was given up to his dream. What did garden parties and baskets and lace frocks matter to him? He was far from all those things. He was wonderful, beautiful. While they were laughing and while the band was playing, this marvel had come to the lane. Happy . . . happy . . . All is well, said that sleeping face. This is just as it should be. I am content.

But all the same you had to cry, and she couldn't go out of the room without saying something to him. Laura gave a loud, childish sob.

"Forgive my hat," she said.

And this time she didn't wait for Em's sister. She found her way out of the door, down the path, past all those dark people. At the corner of the lane she met Laurie. He stepped out of the shadow. "Is that you, Laura?"

"Yes."

"Mother was getting anxious. Was it all right?"

"Yes, quite. Oh, Laurie!" She took his arm, she pressed up against him.

"I say, you're not crying, are you?" asked her brother.

Laura shook her head. She was.

Laurie put his arm round her shoulder. "Don't cry," he said in his warm, loving voice. "Was it awful?"

"No," sobbed Laura. "It was simply marvelous. But Laurie—" She stopped, she looked at her brother. "Isn't life," she stammered, "isn't life—" But what life was she couldn't explain. No matter. He quite understood.

"Isn't it, darling?" said Laurie.

WHAT A TERRIFIC story!

Before the questions, a bit of background. Katherine Mansfield was a writer who came from New Zealand, though she spent all her adult years in England. She produced a sizable handful of very lovely and accomplished stories, and she died young of tuberculosis. There are those who would call her one of the masters of the short story form. "The Garden Party" was published in 1922, the year before she died.

So are you ready for those questions?

First question: What does the story signify?

What is Mansfield saying in the story? What do you see as the story's meaning?

Second question: How does it signify?

What words, ideas, and images does Mansfield use to make her story signify whatever it signifies? What elements, in other words, cause it to mean the things you think it means?

Okay, here are the ground rules.

1. Read carefully.
2. Use any strategies you've picked up from this book or elsewhere to interpret the story.
3. But don't use any sources other than the story itself. (Don't go and read what somebody else, even an English teacher, thinks the story might mean.)
4. No peeking at the rest of this chapter.

5. Write down what you think of. Neatness doesn't count, nor does spelling. Just your observations. Give the story careful thought and write down what you come up with. Then come back and we'll compare notes.

Oh, you're back. That didn't take too long. Not too difficult, I hope?

What I've done in the meantime is to hand the story out to a few college students I happen to know. I'll give you what three of them said and you can see if their thoughts sound familiar.

The first one said, "I know that story. We read it junior year. It's the one about a rich family that lives up on a hill and has no clue about the working class that's trapped down in the valley." This is pretty much what all of the students I talked to noticed. So far, so good. The beauty of this story is that everyone gets it. You feel what's important in it, see the tensions of family and class.

The second one had a little more to say.

To have the party or not, that is the question. Our main character is caught somewhere in between, caught between what is expected of her and how she feels. She faces it. She takes the food, the waste of the party, to the widow in mourning, she faces the horrible reality of humanity. Afterwards, she seeks the comfort of the only person who could possibly understand the situation, her brother, and finds no answers because there are no answers.

That's pretty good. A number of things are beginning to show up here. Both of these readers have picked up what is most central to the story, namely the way that Laura is slowly becoming aware of how class differences and snobbery play a part in her world.

Consider the third response.

What does the story signify?
Mansfield's "The Garden Party" shows the clash between the social classes. More specifically, it shows how people insulate themselves from what lies outside their own narrow view of the world—how to put up blinders (be they with velvet ribbons), if you will.

How does it signify?
Birds and Flight
Mansfield uses the metaphor of birds and flight as a strategy to show how the Sheridans insulate themselves from the lower classes. Jose is a "butterfly." Mrs. Sheridan's voice "floats" and Laura must "skim over the lawn, up the path, up the steps" to reach her. They are all perched high up a "steep rise" from the cottages below. But Laura is a fledgling. Her mother steps back and encourages her to flit around in her preparations for the party, but Laura's wings aren't quite experienced enough—she "flung her arms over her head, took a deep breath, stretched and let them fall," then sighed, so that even a workman "smiled down at her." From her vantage on the ground,

Laura still has a foot in their lower-class world. They are her "neighbors." She has not yet separated herself from them. If Laura is to rise to the level of her family and class, then she is going to need instruction.

Like her siblings before her, she has to learn from her mother. Mrs. Sheridan teaches Laura how to put on a garden party, but more to the point, she teaches the strategy to see the world from a loftier perspective. Like a mother bird teaching her young to fly, Mrs. Sheridan encourages Laura to go so far on her own until it becomes clear that her inexperience requires intervention. When Laura pleads with her mother to cancel the party because of the carter's death, Mrs. Sheridan diverts her with a gift of a new hat.

Laura sees her peers, her fellow partygoers, as "birds that had alighted in the Sheridans' garden for this one afternoon, on their way to—where?" The answer is left vague. There is a danger below at the cottages of the lower classes; when the Sheridan children were young they "were forbidden to set foot there." A man down there has a "house front . . . studded all over with minute birdcages." Those cages represent a threat to the way of life of the high-flying birds of the social elite.

But it is now time for Laura to try her wings. Mrs. Sheridan pushes her from the nest. She tells her to go down to the cottages to give the widow a sympathy basket of their leftovers. Laura faces her conscience. She goes down from the safety of her home, crosses the "broad road" to the cottages, and becomes caged in the house of the dead man. She becomes self-conscious of her appearance, shiny, something apart from the people who live here. She begins to recognize that her world does not belong here, and the realization frightens her. She wants to flee, but she must view the dead man. It is while looking at him that she chooses to see, instead of the reality of the hardship the man's death leaves to his family, an affirmation of her own lifestyle. She reasons that his death has nothing at all to do with "garden parties and baskets and lace frocks," and she is lifted from moral obligation. The revelation is "marvelous." Laura has learned to look at life from a loftier perspective.

WOW. THAT'S NEAT, carefully observed, elegantly expressed. In fact, these three reactions to the story were on the money. If your response was like any of them, give yourself an A.

Now it's my turn.

Think about the title, "The Garden Party." All three students I asked thought about that title too, mostly about its last word, "party." Me, I like the middle one. I like looking at gardens and thinking about them.

What I first notice in the text is that word "ideal." "And after all the weather was ideal." How many times have you described *your* weather as "ideal"? They could not have had a more "perfect" day. The sky is without a cloud. Later, this perfect afternoon will "ripen" and then "slowly fade," as a fruit or flower would. By then we will have seen that the story is full of flowers, as befits a garden party. The roses themselves have bloomed in the hundreds overnight, as if by magic.

When I see an unreal, perfect, almost magical setting like this garden, I generally want to know who's in charge. No mystery here. Everybody does exactly as Mrs. Sheridan says. It is her garden, and what a garden it is, with its hundreds of roses, lily lawn, karaka trees, lavender, plus trays and trays and trays of canna lilies. Mrs. Sheridan believes one cannot have too many canna lilies.

Even the guests become part of her garden realm, seeming to be "bright birds" as they stroll the lawn and stop to admire the flowers. Mrs. Sheridan's hat, which she passes on to Laura, has "gold daisies." Clearly she is the queen or goddess of this garden world.

Food is also something Mrs. Sheridan rules over. She is responsible for the food for the party, sandwiches (fifteen different kinds) and cream puffs and passion-fruit ices. And she rules over her children, of which she has four. So, a queen overseeing her realm of plants, food, and children. Mrs. Sheridan begins to sound suspiciously like a fertility goddess. Since, however, there are lots of kinds of fertility goddesses, we need more information.

I'm not done with that hat. It's a black hat with black velvet ribbons and gold daisies, equally out of place at the party and at the house of the dead man. But I'm less impressed by what the hat is than by whose it is. Mrs. Sheridan bought it, but she insists that Laura take it, declaring it "much too young" for herself. Although Laura resists, she does accept the hat and is later captivated by her own "charming" image in the mirror.

No doubt she does look charming, but part of her charm is borrowed. When a younger character takes on an older character's talisman, an object of power and importance, then she also takes on some of that older character's power. This is true whether it's a father's coat, a mentor's sword, a teacher's pen, or a mother's hat.

Because the hat came from Mrs. Sheridan, Laura instantly becomes more closely associated with her mother than any of her other siblings. She is the one who stands beside her mother as the party guests say their good-byes. She is the one sent with the basket her mother has filled with leftovers.

Let's look at Laura's trip. The perfect afternoon on the high hill is ending and "growing dusky as Laura shut[s] their garden gates." From here on her trip grows darker and darker. The cottages down in the hollow are in "deep shade," the lane "smoky and dark." She wishes she had put a coat on, since her bright frock shines amid the dismal surroundings. Inside the dead man's house itself, she goes down "a gloomy passage" to a kitchen "lighted by a smoky lamp." When her visit ends, she makes her way past "all those dark people" to a spot where her brother, Laurie, steps "out of the shadow."

There are a couple of odd things to notice here. For one thing, on her way to the lane, Laura sees a large dog "running by like a shadow." Upon getting to the bottom, she crosses the "broad road" to go into the dismal lane. Once in the lane, there's an old, old woman with a crutch sitting with her feet on the newspaper. When the old woman says the house is indeed that of the dead man, she "smiles queerly." Although Laura hasn't wanted to see the dead man, when the sheets are folded back, she finds him "wonderful, beautiful." Laurie, it turns out, has come to wait at the end of the lane—almost as if he can't enter—because "Mother was getting quite anxious."

What just happened?

For one thing, as my students note, Laura has seen how the other half lives—and dies. One major point of the story is the way she meets the lower class and the challenges that throws at her easy class assumptions and prejudices. And then there is the story of a young girl growing up, part of which involves seeing her first dead man. But I think something else is going on here.

I think Laura has just gone to hell.

Hades, actually. The classical underworld, the realm of the dead.

Not only that, she hasn't gone as Laura Sheridan, but as Persephone. I know what you're thinking: *now he's lost his mind*. It wouldn't be the first time and possibly not the last.

Persephone's mother is Demeter, the goddess of agriculture, fertility, and marriage. Food, flowers, children. Does that sound like anyone we know?

Now here's the quick version of the myth: Demeter has a beautiful daughter, Persephone. Persephone is kidnapped by Hades, the god of the underworld, who wants to marry her. While in the underworld with him, she eats six pomegranate seeds. Anyone who tastes a bite of food in the underworld is doomed to stay there, so it seems that Persephone will be stuck with Hades forever. But her mother is miserable about losing her daughter, and when the goddess of all growing things is miserable, the whole earth feels it. Plants wither and die. Nothing flowers or bears fruit. Everyone might starve. The other gods step in and hammer out a bargain: six months a year in the underworld for Persephone, one month for every pomegranate seed she ate. Six months aboveground with her mother. So when Persephone is with Demeter, we have summer, sunshine, growth, and harvest. When Persephone is underground again, we have fall, winter, cold, and barren fields.

What we get here, of course, is the myth explaining the turning of the seasons, and what sort of culture would fail to have a myth explaining that? But that's not the only thing this myth covers. There's also the idea of a young woman arriving at adulthood, and this is a huge step, since it includes facing and coming to understand death.

So how does that make Laura into Persephone, you ask? First, there's her mother as Demeter. That's pretty obvious, I think, once the flowers and food and children are considered. And you should also remember that they live high up on a hill—a bit like Mount Olympus, where Demeter and the other Greek gods dwell.

Then there is the trip down the hill and into a world full of shadows and smoke and darkness. Laura crosses the broad road as if it were the River Styx, which you must cross to enter Hades. To get into the underworld, you must make your way past the three-headed guard dog, Cerberus, and you must have the ticket of admission. (For the Trojan hero Aeneas, that ticket was the Golden Bough, a tree branch with golden leaves.) Oh, and a guide wouldn't hurt. Laura meets the dog just outside her garden gate, and her Golden Bough turns out to be the daisies on her hat. As for a guide, Laura has the old woman with the queer smile. And Laura's deep admiration of the dead man suggests a kind of symbolic marriage. Laura, like Persephone, has been joined to the underworld, the world of the dead.

Okay, so *why* all this business from three or four thousand years ago? That's what you're wondering, right? There are a couple of reasons.

Remember, the Persephone myth is about a young woman stepping into her adult life. To do that, she has to understand sex (she gets married) and death (she journeys to the underworld). Laura admires the workmen who arrive to put up the marquee, liking them better than the young men who come to Sunday supper, suitors of her sisters. Later she finds the dead man beautiful—a response that involves both death and sex. At the end of the story, she struggles to tell Laurie something about life but cannot finish her sentence. "Isn't life—" she stammers. She is so deeply involved in the world of the dead that she cannot, at the moment, make any kind of statement about life. In tapping into this ancient tale of a young woman's journey into adult life, Mansfield gives Laura's story the power of the myth itself.

When Persephone returns from the world of the dead, she has in a sense *become* her mother. Some Greek rituals treated Persephone and Demeter as if they were the same. That may be a good thing if your mother is really Demeter. It's not so good if she is Mrs. Sheridan. Wearing her mother's hat, carrying her mother's basket, Laura also takes on her mother's views. Although Laura struggles against her family's snobbery throughout the story, she cannot really escape from it. When she is relieved to see Laurie at the end, relieved to return home, that shows how her attempts to become her own person and think her own thoughts are not completely successful. It's something we can all recognize from our own lives. Who can deny that there is a good deal of our parents in us, for good or ill?

What if you don't see all this as going on in the story? What if you read it simply as a tale of a young woman making an ill-advised trip on which she learns something about her world? Then that's fine. It's a quest! First of all, the story has to work simply by telling us what happens to Laura. Understanding that is a great starting point.

From there, if you consider the pattern of images in the story (flowers, summer, light, perfection, darkness, shadows, dogs, dead bodies), you'll begin to see more going on. Maybe your ideas will not resemble mine or the other students I quoted here. But if you're reading carefully and consider all the possibilities, you'll find ideas of your own that will deepen your experience of the story.

So what does the story signify, then? Many things. It criticizes the class system. It's a story of a young woman stepping into the adult world of sex and death. It's an amusing look at family relationships. It's a touching portrait of a child struggling to grow into an independent person in the face of strong, nearly overwhelming influence from a parent.

What else could we ask of such a simple little story?

ENVOI

THERE'S A VERY old tradition in poetry of adding a little stanza, shorter than the rest, at the end of a long poem or a book of poems. This ritual sending-off was called the "envoi." The French word it comes from, *envoyer,* is a verb that means, more or less, to send off on a mission.

In that same manner, I have a few thoughts with which to send you on your way.

First, a confession and a warning. If I have given the impression somehow (by getting to the end of the book, for example) that I've told you everything there is to know about how literature can be written or understood, then I apologize. It simply isn't true. In fact, we've only scratched the surface here.

How could I have forgotten to mention fire, for

example? Somehow it just didn't come up. There are dozens of other topics we could have covered. No writer could include them all, and no reader would want to plow through them. I'm pretty sure I could have made this book twice as long. I'm also pretty sure neither of us wants that.

So this is not a list of all the codes and references that writers and readers use when they create and understand literature. Instead it's an outline. A pattern. A guide to help you learn to look for those codes on your own.

Second, you're lucky. All those other codes? You don't need them. At least you don't need them all spelled out. There comes a point in anybody's reading when watching for pattern and symbols becomes nearly automatic. You'll just start to notice when words and images are calling out for attention.

You can figure out fire. Or horses. Characters in stories have ridden horses for thousands of years. What does it mean to be mounted on a horse instead of being on foot? Think about it: Diomedes and Odysseus stealing the Thracian horses in *The Iliad*, the Lone Ranger waving from astride the rearing Silver, Richard III crying out for a horse, Dennis Hopper and Peter Fonda roaring down the road on their motorcycles in *Easy Rider*. What do we understand about horses and riding them or driving them—or not? See? You can do it just fine.

Third, some suggestions. In the appendix, I offer some ideas for further reading. There's nothing too organized about these ideas. I'm certainly not suggesting you have to read exactly these books and no others. Mostly these are books I've mentioned along the way, books I like and admire, books I think you might like as well.

My main suggestion, though, is to read things you like. You're not stuck with my list. Go to your bookstore or library and find novels, plays, stories that connect with your imagination and intelligence. Much of what I like best in my reading I've found by accident as I poked around bookshelves. Your reading should be fun. It's all a form of play. So play, Dear Reader, play.

And fare thee well.

READING LIST

I'VE TOSSED BOOK and poem titles at you, sometimes at a dizzying pace. This kind of thing can make you feel excited, so you go on to read more books, or infuriated, so you blame the authors and books you never heard of for making you feel dumb. Never feel dumb. Not knowing about a book or author simply shows what you haven't gotten to yet. I find more works and writers every day that I haven't gotten to, haven't even heard of.

What I offer here is a list of books mentioned throughout the book, plus some others I probably should have mentioned, or would have if I had more chapters to write. What all these works have in common is that a reader can learn a lot from them. I have learned a lot from them.

I do not claim that these books are better than other books I have not chosen, or that *The Iliad* is better than Charles Dickens. I do have strong opinions about which books are better and why, but that's not what this is about. All I can claim for these books is that, if you read them, you will become more learned. That's it. We're in the learning business. I am, and if you've read this far, so are you. Education is about classes and grades; learning is what we do for ourselves. When we're lucky, they go together. If I had to choose, I'd take learning.

Oh, there's another thing that will happen if you read the books on this list: you will have a good time, mostly. I promise. Hey, I can't guarantee that everyone will like everything or that my taste is your taste. What I can guarantee is that these books are entertaining. We speak of literary *works,* but in fact literature is mostly play. If you read novels and plays and stories and poems and you're not having fun, somebody is doing something wrong. If a novel seems like a struggle, quit; you're not getting paid to read it, are you? And you surely won't get fired if you don't read it. So enjoy.

PRIMARY WORKS

Louisa May Alcott, *Little Women* (1868–1869). The lives of four sisters, and the death of one.

W. H. Auden, "Musée des Beaux Arts" (1940). A meditation on human suffering, based on a Pieter

Brueghel painting. There's a lot more great Auden where this came from.

Samuel Beckett, *Waiting for Godot* (1954). What if there's a road but characters don't travel it? Would that mean something?

Libba Bray, *Beauty Queens* (2011). Might make you take a second look at all those TV commercials for clothes, shampoo, and makeup, and wonder what exactly you're being sold. Plus it's extremely funny.

Frances Hodgson Burnett, *A Little Princess* (1905) and ***The Secret Garden*** (1911). These might seem a bit old-fashioned, but they were some of the first books for young readers to give us real children (sometimes bad, sometimes good, always interesting) instead of paper cutouts who were rewarded for virtues and punished for vices.

Geoffrey Chaucer, *The Canterbury Tales* (1384). You'll have to read this one in a modern translation unless you've had training in Middle English, but it's wonderful in any language. Funny, heartbreaking, warm, ironic, everything a diverse group of people traveling together and telling stories is likely to be.

Robert Cormier, *The Chocolate War* (1974). Not all readers are comfortable with Cormier's dark view of the world—but people with power often use it badly, and you won't find a more honest look at this harsh truth.

Roald Dahl, *Charlie and the Chocolate Factory*

(1964). In Dahl's world, humor lives alongside a fierce kind of judgment about human nature—it's entertaining and a little unnerving. Good stuff.

Charles Dickens, *A Christmas Carol* (1843). Dickens is the most humane writer you'll ever read. He believes in people, even with all their faults, and he slings a great story, with the most memorable characters you'll meet anywhere.

Sharon M. Draper, *Romiette and Julio* (1999). If *West Side Story* isn't enough for you, look here for another way to retell Shakespeare's classic story.

Neil Gaiman, *The Graveyard Book* (2008). Funny, scary, and clever.

William Golding, *Lord of the Flies* (1954). You'll never look at recess the same way again.

Lorraine Hansberry, *A Raisin in the Sun* (1959). Race, class, and family, all in one tightly written play.

Ernest Hemingway, *A Farewell to Arms* (1929) and ***The Old Man and the Sea*** (1952).

Homer, *The Iliad* and ***The Odyssey*** (from the eighth century B.C.). The second of these is probably easier going for modern readers, but they're both great. Every time I teach *The Iliad,* I have students who say, "I had no idea this was such a great story."

Victor Hugo, *The Hunchback of Notre Dame* (1831).

Washington Irving, "Rip Van Winkle" (1819). Irving was one of the earliest writers to think carefully about what it means to be American.

Henry James, "Daisy Miller" (1878). It's about the way human beings consume one another.

Rudyard Kipling, *The Jungle Book* (1894) and ***The Second Jungle Book*** (1895).

C. S. Lewis, *The Lion, the Witch and the Wardrobe* (1950).

Stephenie Meyer, *Twilight* (2005). You don't need me to tell you to take a look at this one, right?

Edgar Allan Poe, "The Fall of the House of Usher" (1839) and **"The Masque of the Red Death"** (1842). Poe's stories (and poems, for that matter) have the logic of our nightmares, the terror of thoughts we can't suppress or control.

J. K. Rowling, *Harry Potter and the Sorcerer's Stone* (1997). You don't need me here either. Continue through rest of series.

William Shakespeare (1564–1616). Take your pick. Here's mine: ***Hamlet, Romeo and Juliet, Julius Caesar, Macbeth*, *King Lear*, *Henry V*, *A Midsummer Night's Dream*, *Much Ado about Nothing*, *The Tempest*, *A Winter's Tale*, *As You Like It*, *Twelfth Night*.** And then there are the sonnets. Read all of them you can. Hey, they're only fourteen lines long. I particularly like Sonnet 73, but there are a lot of wonderful sonnets in there.

Mary Shelley, *Frankenstein* (1818). The monster isn't simply monstrous. He says something about his creator and about the society in which Victor Frankenstein lives.

Sophocles, *Oedipus Rex, Oedipus at Colonus*, and ***Antigone*** (fifth century B.C.). These plays make up a trilogy dealing with a doomed family. The first (which is the first really great detective story in Western literature) is about blindness and vision, the second about traveling on the road and the place where all roads end, and the third a meditation on power, loyalty to the state, and personal morality. These plays, now over twenty-four hundred years old, never go out of style.

Robert Louis Stevenson, *The Strange Case of Dr. Jekyll and Mr. Hyde* (1886). Stevenson does fascinating things with the possibilities of the divided self (the one with a good and an evil side).

Bram Stoker, *Dracula* (1897). What, you need a reason?

Dr. Seuss, *Green Eggs and Ham* (1960) and ***How the Grinch Stole Christmas*** (1957). If you somehow missed out on these in your early childhood, I'm very sorry. Go back and read them now.

Theodore Taylor, *The Cay* (1969). A short book with a lot packed into it—childhood, growing up, race and racism, war, survival.

Mark Twain, *Adventures of Huckleberry Finn* (1885). Poor Huck has come under attack in recent decades, and yes, it does have that racist word in it (not surprising for a work depicting a racist society), but *Huck Finn* has more sheer humanity than any three books I can think of. And it's one of the great road-buddy stories of all time, even if the road is soggy.

Eudora Welty, "Why I Live at the P.O." (1941). Family, family, family—how we get along and how we don't.

Laura Ingalls Wilder, the Little House series. What family means and what frontier means—two great questions to ponder.

FAIRY TALES WE CAN'T LIVE WITHOUT

"Sleeping Beauty," "Snow White," "Hansel and Gretel," "Rapunzel," "Rumpelstiltskin."

MOVIES TO READ

The Gold Rush (1925) and ***Modern Times*** (1936). Charlie Chaplin is the greatest film comedian ever. Accept no substitutes.

Notorious (1946), ***North by Northwest*** (1959), and ***Psycho*** (1960). Somebody's always copying Hitchcock. Meet the original.

O Brother, Where Art Thou? (2000). Not only a reworking of *The Odyssey* but an excellent road-buddy film with a great American soundtrack.

Pale Rider (1985). Clint Eastwood's fullest treatment of his mythic avenging-angel hero.

Raiders of the Lost Ark (1981), ***Indiana Jones and the Temple of Doom*** (1984), and ***Indiana Jones***

and the Last Crusade (1989). Great quest stories. You know when you're searching for the lost Ark of the Covenant or the Holy Grail that you're dealing with quests. Take away Indy's leather jacket, fedora, and whip and give him chain mail, helmet, and lance, and see if he doesn't look considerably like Sir Gawain.

Star Wars (1977), ***The Empire Strikes Back*** (1981), and ***Return of the Jedi*** (1983). George Lucas's trilogy does a great job of showing us types of heroes and villains. If you know the Arthurian legends, so much the better. Personally, I don't care if you learn anything about all that from the films or not; they're so much fun, you deserve to see them. Repeatedly.

West Side Story (1957). Tony and Maria, the Jets and the Sharks, plus some of the best song and dance a musical ever offered.

ACKNOWLEDGMENTS

IT IS IMPOSSIBLE to thank individually all the students who have had a hand in creating this book, and yet it couldn't have come into being without them. Their constant prompting, doubting, questioning, answering, suggesting, and responding drove me to figure out most of the ideas and observations that have gone into these essays. Their patience with my wacky notions is often astonishing, their willingness to try on difficult ideas and perplexing works gratifying. For every routine comment or piercing query, every bright idea or dull-eyed stare, every wisecrack of theirs or groan at one of mine, every laugh or snarl, every statement praising or dismissing a literary work, I am profoundly grateful. They never let me rest or become complacent. Several students in particular have had a hand in the development of this book, and I wish to single them out for special thanks. Monica Mann's smart-aleck comment pointed out to me that I have quite a number of little aphorisms about literature, although even then it took several years for me to see the possibilities in the "Quotations of Chairman Tom," as she called them. Mary Ann Halboth has listened to and commented on much of what became the material of this study, often pushing my ideas well beyond my initial conceptions. Kelly Tobeler and Diane Saylor agreed to be guinea pigs for certain experiments and offered insightful, amazing interpretations of the Katherine Mansfield story; their contributions made my final chapter immeasurably better.

I am deeply indebted to numerous colleagues for their assistance, insight, encouragement, and patience. I especially wish to thank Professors Frederic Svoboda, Stephen Bernstein, Mary Jo Kietzman, and Jan Furman, who read drafts, provided ideas and information, listened to my complaints and obsessions, and offered support and wisdom. Their intelligence, good humor, and generosity have made my efforts lighter and the product greatly improved. To have such brilliant and dedicated colleagues is a genuine gift. They make me sound much smarter than I am. Of course that's not too hard. The errors, however, are purely my own.

To my agent, Faith Hamlin, and her assistant, Kate

Darling, and to my editor at HarperCollins, Nikola Scott, many thanks for their belief in the work, as well as for all their many constructive criticisms and suggestions.

As ever, I with to thank my family for their support, patience, and love. My sons, Robert and Nathan, read chapters, contributed interpretations, and gave me firsthand insights into the student mind. My wife, Brenda, took care of worldly and mundane tasks so that I could lose myself in the writing. To all three I offer my immense gratitude and love.

And finally I wish to thank my muse. After all these years of reading and writing, I still don't understand where inspiration comes from, but I am profoundly grateful that it keeps coming.

INDEX

G

H

I

J

M

S